Simple Internet

Jeffrey M. Cogswell

WAITE GROUP PRESS™

Corte Madera, CA

Publisher: **Mitchell Waite**
Editor-in-Chief: **Scott Calamar**
Editorial Director: **Joel Fugazzotto**
Managing Editor: **Dan Scherf**
Content Editor: **Marianne Krcma**
Copy Editor: **Judith Brown**
Technical Reviewer: **Miko Matsumora**
Production Director: **Julianne Ososke**
Design: **Karen Johnston**
Production: **Jamie Sue Brooks**
Back Cover and Interior Illustrations: **Neal Adam's Trans Continuity Studios in Burbank, CA**
Cover Design: **Michael Rogondino**
Front Cover Illustration: **Steve Vance**

Printed in the United States of America
95 96 97 • 10 9 8 7 6 5 4 3 2

Cogswell, Jeffrey M., 1968–
Simple Internet/Jeffrey Cogswell.
    p.   cm.
At head of title: The Waite Group.
Includes index.
ISBN: 1-878739-79-4: $16.95
1. Internet (Computer network)   I. Waite Group.   II. Title.
TK5105.875.I57C63 1994
004.6'7—dc20

Dedication

This book is dedicated to all the musicians whose works have so greatly influenced my creativity.

About the Author

Jeff Cogswell has been programming computers since his teenage days with Pet computer and VIC-20s. Since then, he has taught and tutored numerous students in areas including Mathematics and Computer Science. He is a full-time writer and computer consultant. He has written for various computer magazines, including *Windows Tech Journal* and *Dr. Dobb's Journal*. When he's not writing or programming, he spends his time playing jazz piano and the electric guitar and credits Rachmaninoff and Eddie Van Halen as his influences.

Table of Contents

Contents

Contents

Dear Reader,

What is a book? Is it perpetually fated to be inky words on a paper page? Or can a book simply be something that inspires—feeding your head with ideas and creativity regardless of the medium? The latter, I believe. That's why I'm always pushing our books to a higher plane; using new technology to reinvent the medium.

I wrote my first book in 1973, *Projects in Sights, Sounds, and Sensations*. I like to think of it as our first multimedia book. In the years since then, I've learned that people want to *experience* information, not just passively absorb it—they want interactive MTV in a book. With this in mind, I started my own publishing company and published **Master C**, a book/disk package that turned the PC into a C language instructor. Then we branched out to computer graphics with **Fractal Creations,** which included a color poster, 3-D glasses, and a totally rad fractal generator. Ever since, we've included disks and other goodies with most of our books. **Virtual Reality Creations** is bundled with 3-D Fresnel viewing goggles and **Walkthroughs & Flybys CD** comes with a multimedia CD-ROM. We've made complex multimedia accessible for any PC user with **Ray Tracing Creations**, **Multimedia Creations**, **Making Movies on Your PC**, **Image Lab**, and three books on Fractals.

The Waite Group continues to publish innovative multimedia books on cutting-edge topics, and of course the programming books that make up our heritage. Being a programmer myself, I appreciate clear guidance through a tricky OS, so our books come bundled with disks and CDs loaded with code, utilities, and custom controls.

By 1995, The Waite Group will have published 150 books. Our next step is to develop a new type of book, an interactive, multimedia experience involving the reader on many levels.

With this new book, you'll be trained by a computer-based instructor with infinite patience, run a simulation to visualize the topic, play a game that shows you different aspects of the subject, interact with others on-line, and have instant access a large database on the subject. For traditionalists, there will be a full-color, paper-based book.

In the meantime, they've wired the White House for hi-tech; the information super highway has been proposed; and computers, communication, entertainment, and information are becoming inseparable. To travel in this Digital Age you'll need guidebooks. The Waite Group offers such guidance for the most important software—your mind.

We hope you enjoy this book. For a color catalog, just fill out and send in the Reader Report Card at the back of the book.

Sincerely,

Mitchell Waite

Mitchell Waite
Publisher

WAITE
GROUP
PRESS™

Acknowledgments

As with any book, there are far more people involved than just the author. I'd like to personally thank the following people for helping out.

First, thanks to everyone at Waite Group Press, as well as all the hired editors who helped out. Special thanks to Dan Scherf for doing an excellent job; thanks to John Crudo for all the moral support; and thanks to Marianne Krcma for the content edits and wonderful suggestions. Thanks to Mitch Waite and Scott Calamar for all the creative ideas.

Thanks to my brothers, Joel Cogswell and Steve Cogswell. Joel was learning to use the Internet as I was writing this book, and he gave me some really good ideas on how to present the different material. Steve rescued me towards the end when I was suddenly unable to log in just days before the manuscript was due. He helped me get back online.

Thanks to all the folks who talked Internet with me: Tom Salzmann for helping me stomp on the modem and for getting me a UUCP connection, Michelle Vallery for finding articles and helping me research, Randy Hamilton, John Robbins, and Mark Darling. Mark also took the picture of me for my first book, *Simple C++*. Thanks to Scott Yanoff for providing an excellent list of Internet sites. Thanks also to Jeannette Duckworth for providing moral support and helping me stay in a good mood.

Thanks to all my teachers over the years, especially those who have helped my writing, including Mrs. Nancy Engemann and Miss Ester Hall.

Thanks to all the musicians whose music helped keep my creativity going. In particular, I found terrific inspiration from Peter Gabriel's *So* and *Us* CDs; Roger Waters' *Amused to Death*; David Lanz and Paul Speer's *Bridge of Dreams*; and Alan Parson Project's *Gaudi*. The completion of this book coincided with the release of Pink Floyd's astounding CD *The Division Bell*, and the final writing of the Introduction coincided with Pink Floyd's performance in Chapel Hill, NC, on the day of a solar eclipse.

Finally, very special thanks to my creative friends, especially Trish Rucker, Lisa Whittington, Heather Russell, and Kelly O'Connor.

Introduction

One day I walked into a bookstore that specializes in computer books, and I began chatting with a college student working there. I mentioned my first book, *Simple C++*, was due out soon, and I wondered if they had it on order yet. We got to talking about writing, and I mentioned I was writing a book called *Simple Internet*. The man looked at me funny and said, "That's a contradiction of terms!" I laughed and agreed and walked out.

When I got home, I thought about what he'd said. I was already writing a book that was supposed to disprove that, but could it be disproven?

There is a lot to the Internet. And there are parts of it that alone can make you feel like you need a Ph.D. in Computer Science to understand. But the more I used the Internet, the more I realized it didn't have to be that difficult. It is mostly a matter of understanding *what* is happening *when*. If you understand that, the rest comes together quite nicely.

This book, then, is the result of my own fight to understand the Internet. In the spirit of my first book, *Simple C++*, it takes you through a story. Here, our hero, Archie Finger, Private Eye, must solve a mystery of finding a missing person. While doing so, he is forced to learn and understand the Internet. And he discovers it's really not that bad, after all.

This book starts you out from the very beginning of using the Internet. But while other books spend time explaining the history of the Internet, and while those books assume you're sitting at a computer that's directly linked to the Internet, this book explains the process of dialing into an Internet provider and shows some cool stuff that's out there.

What You Need to Begin

You will need a computer, a modem, and what's known as a terminal program. The terminal program helps you use your modem. Fortunately, most modems come with a terminal program. Many computers and operating systems come with terminal programs, too. For instance, Microsoft Windows comes with a terminal program called TERMINAL.

You will also need to know how to use your terminal program; there are far too many of them to cover here. When there is a reference in this book to information that's specific to a terminal program, I've noted that yours may be different, but suggested keystrokes or menu items that might work. You need to know how to start your terminal program and how to dial out. For many terminal programs, you either choose a menu called Dial, or press (ALT)-(D). Or you might simply type **ATDT**, followed by a space, followed by the phone number, and then press (ENTER). You also need to know how to download files. Again, there's generally a menu item called Download, or a keystroke, such as (PAGE DOWN). There are also other things you may want to know about your terminal program, such as how to hang up. For many programs, there's either a Hangup menu item, or a Disconnect menu item, or a keystroke, such as (ALT)-(H).

Another thing you'll need is an account with an Internet provider. Fortunately, these are becoming more and more common. One place to start looking is at the ads in the Business section of your Sunday paper. If there are any local Internet providers, they probably advertise there. If your area has a local newspaper devoted to the computer business, there are probably ads there, too. There are also large online services that provide Internet access to people all over the country; these services generally advertise in the national computer magazines. Some of these magazines have advertiser indexes according to topic as well as name, so you may find them there. Beware of some providers who claim they give you "Internet access!" Some only give you a few of the capabilities, such as email. It may help to ask a knowledgeable friend or two. Whatever provider you end up with, it should include things called telnet, network news, and ftp. (We'll look at these later in the book.)

That's about all you'll need! This book takes you through the rest.

Let's Get Started

There's a lot of cool stuff waiting out there on the Internet for you. Unfortunately, computers come and go, new things are added and removed almost daily, and that makes it nearly impossible to guarantee that everything listed in this book will still be there by the time you read it. Fortunately, though, in this book you'll also see ways to find new stuff that's out there; stuff that isn't listed in this book.

That's it for now. Get ready for a really cool mystery while you learn how to use the Internet. Have fun!

CHAPTER 1

A Message from Afar

The night wind howled. Archie looked around the dark room nervously; then he looked at Veronica. She stood beside him, holding the candle near her face. He could see her eyes glancing back and forth, back and forth.

They heard the rain begin.

"And to think," whispered Veronica, "when we came in here only a few minutes ago, all was quiet and clear."

"The bad weather sure moved in quickly," added Archie.

He heard the shutters slam shut in the wind. They opened again, then slammed again, opened and closed, opened and closed.

"This house has no shutters," whispered Veronica.

Archie looked around the room again. "Oh, wait a minute," he said. "I see the problem." He walked to the coffee table, reached down, and pressed the stop button on the remote control. The storm stopped and the room was suddenly quiet.

"That's better," said Veronica, laughing a bit. She reached over and turned on a lamp.

"Sure, but I wonder where the TV is that we heard?" Archie looked at a cabinet and spotted the cable box on top of it. "Well, the cable box is over there. Maybe the TV's inside the cabinet."

Veronica walked over and opened that cabinet. Sure enough. That's where the TV was. "Well," she said, "we just solved our first mystery for the evening. Too bad it's the wrong one."

Discovering the Internet

"I guess if we're gonna find this missing person, we better start looking for clues." Archie wandered slowly around the room. He was observing a couple of photos on a shelf as he said somewhat distantly, "So your friend who owns this place vanished the day before last. You sure he didn't just go out of town?"

"Yes, I'm sure. He would have told me, since I've been coming over every day to work on the computer."

Archie noticed a Ming vase with no flowers in it. "How did he get so rich?"

"I think he owns his own business."

"What does he do?"

"I'm not sure. Something to do with computers. Consulting, maybe."

"Hmmmm . . ." Archie decided to give up on this room. He headed for the hallway, and noticed a den. He turned on the light and entered. Inside was a computer. He approached the computer, which was off. Sitting by the computer was a blank pad of paper.

Archie chuckled quietly to himself as he remembered something he saw on TV. It might have been one of those old detective shows from the early 1970s when Archie was just a kid, but he wasn't sure—maybe it was the "Rockford Files." He grabbed the top piece of paper off the pad and held it at different angles to allow the light to shine on it in different ways.

Finally he could see something.

"What's that?"

He nearly jumped through the ceiling. "Don't sneak up on me like that when we're rummaging through some guy's house," he said to Veronica.

"Sorry," she said. She looked at the paper. "Hey, I saw someone do that once on TV. I think it was the Hardy Boys. Or was it Nancy Drew?"

"I don't remember." Suddenly the angle was right. "Aha!" He could see something. It was the indentation from something previously written on a sheet atop this sheet. Although a couple of letters weren't quite visible, it looked something like this:

owner@super.geeks.com

Odd, thought Archie. What would that mean? He grabbed another sheet of paper and wrote down what he could see. "Does this mean anything to you?" he asked Veronica.

She looked it over. "Looks like an Internet address."

"What's the Internet?"

"It's an enormous collection of computers all hooked together across the world. If a person is sitting in, say, California, at a computer hooked into the Internet, he or she can type something and have it appear within minutes on the screen of a computer on the other side of the planet. Sometimes it takes longer, even hours, but it's still pretty amazing."

"Hmm. Sort of reminds me of one of those services I used to use when I was growing up, where you had a computer and you could hook up your phone to it and call some phone number. Then your computer would be connected to other computers across the country, and people could talk to each other by typing on their keyboards."

"Yeah," said Veronica, "it sort of works like that, only a lot better. There are lots more things the Internet can do. We'll see more in later chapters."

"Huh?"

"Oh, sorry, sometimes I feel like I'm living in a book."

"That's okay, sometimes I feel like I'm living in a movie."

"So this thing is an Internet address," said Veronica.

"How'd you get so smart? I'm supposed to be the private investigator here. Go on."

"An *Internet address* is a unique name and location identifying somebody on the Internet. When someone sends a message, called a piece of *email* (pronounced 'ee-mail') out over the Internet, they need to specify where to send the message. The 'where' is what's known as an Internet address. Every person who's connected to a computer system has his or her own unique identifier, and that's their address. By specifying this unique Internet address, you ensure the message goes to the proper computer system, and ultimately, the proper person, or *user,* as computer people like to call them."

Archie walked over to the bookshelf. There were piles and piles of computer books. "I guess this guy is quite the computer geek. Look at all this stuff. Half the titles have words in them I've never even seen. Archie pulled down one rather thick book. It was called *Everything You Wanted to Know About the Internet (and Then Some).* He paged through it, and saw what must have been ten-syllable words. A couple pages even had math formulas on them! Now *that's* scary, thought Archie. "This book explains the Internet," he said. "Or, it looks like it *tries* to anyway. Looks like a college textbook. Seems like somebody could write a better one for us regular people to read."

He put the book back on the shelf. Forget that huge thing. He looked around the room some more, and noticed a trapdoor. Veronica was looking at it, but he didn't want her to explore it. The last thing he needed was for this simple little mystery about a missing person to turn into some underworld action-packed adventure. Who knows where that trapdoor led?

She was opening it. He grabbed the book and threw it towards the trapdoor. It landed smack on the trapdoor, and was so heavy the door slammed shut with a loud bang.

"Hey! What are you doing?"

"Check out that book."

She paged through it. "Wow, this is cool."

"Sure, if you can read it. But I only have a Ph.D. in accounting. I guess I'm not smart enough, huh?"

"Oh, stop it," she said. "This could be helpful. Let's take it with us."

"Um, we better not steal anything. Don't want to get in trouble. As it is, if you didn't have keys to this place, we'd be breaking and entering."

"Remember, the missing person is a friend of mine. We'll return it after we find him. And I'll just say he loaned it to me. In fact, when we find him I'll tell him to tell people that. He will. He's a good friend."

"Ohhhh, okay. I think we found enough clues to get us started. Let's go back to the office. And don't forget it's a school night. We both have to be back to work in the morning, at our real daytime jobs."

"But let's see where this trapdoor goes first," she said. "I've noticed it the times I've been here, and I've always wondered . . ."

"Let's not. There might be bats or rats or something."

"Oh, nonsense." She opened it. There was a small opening under it, only about a foot deep. She pulled out a large chalice. "Check this out!" she said.

"Oh, that's just the Holy Grail. Put it back. Don't wanna break it."

She laughed. "Wouldn't that be funny if it really was the Holy Grail?" She started to return it to its proper place, but as she did it slipped out of her fingers.

Archie saw the whole thing and cringed as it made a shattering sound. "Ooohhh," he groaned.

"No," she said, "that wouldn't be funny. We'd better get out of here."

They hurried for the door.

Operation Internet Entry: Getting On

Outside, the weather was chilly. The night sky was clear, and the stars were shining brightly. They climbed into the car and headed for the office, which was actually in Archie's house. Their little side business didn't yet generate enough income to afford a real office.

On the way there, they chatted more about the Internet.

"So this Internet thing," said Archie, "is some gigantic computer network? Like all these computer systems all hooked together?"

"Basically, yeah."

"So like if I'm working at one computer in, say, the Pentagon, and I want to send a message to, say, someone in NASA in Florida, I could?"

"Sure."

"So why don't I just pick up the phone and call?"

"Because you may have really long messages, or you may need to send a copy of a computer program or a word processor file or something. Or you might just prefer to say it in writing."

"So what else can you do?"

"Well, let's see." She opened up the book.

He reached over and closed it. "Don't bother with that thing. I'd rather speak English, not computerese, or whatever."

"Okay, okay. I'm no expert, but as I understand it, there are daily messages coming to all computers, for everyone to read. They come from all different places. You can even post messages for everyone to read. It's called *network news*. There are also ways to connect to many of the different computers all over the Internet. You can get programs from them or use their online services. For instance, many libraries are adding Internet services, so you can actually connect to their computers from anywhere on the planet, as long as you have Internet access. Then you can look up books in their electronic card catalog, and you might even be able to have the book sent to a local library over interlibrary loan. Another thing you can do is talk to other people over the Internet—as they type things on their computer, the words appear on their own screen and yours too; and when you type, everything appears on your screen and theirs too."

"So how do we get on this Internet thing, so I can actually see for myself what it is?"

"Well, we can talk to the computer nerd at work. Maybe he can get our computers at work hooked in. But that would probably take a couple months."

"Well, our missing person will probably be found by then, so we don't have that much time. We wanna be the first to find him. Otherwise it'd spoil all the fun."

"I think I heard about some local computer that's on the Internet that we can have our computers dial into over phone lines. We won't be able to do everything, but we can still do an awful lot. They're actually a local private company that offers it as a service. All you need is a credit card."

"My cards are all maxed out. Ahem . . ."

"Okay, okay, we'll use mine. We need to get hold of one of their ads. Let's stop up there at the 24-hour grocery store. There's a local computer newspaper that probably has ads for the service. Lots of big cities have these kinds of newspapers, and if there's a local service, they might advertise there."

"What about," asked Archie, "our readers who don't have a local computer newspaper?"

"There are some places they can write to or call that might help. Also, there are a couple of dial-in services that offer Internet hookup from pretty much anywhere in the country. One is called Delphi. It's a big service out of Cambridge, Massachusetts."

They stopped at the grocery store and found a newspaper with an ad for a local Internet connection that looked like Figure 1-1.

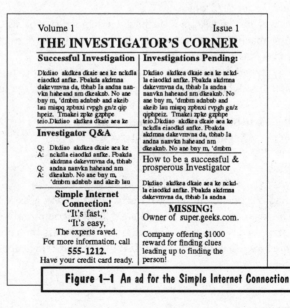

Figure 1-1 An ad for the Simple Internet Connection

"This one looks pretty good," said Veronica, as they stood outside the grocery store munching on bagels at two in the morning. "Looks like we can dial in tonight, right from the office computer."

"I'm tired," said Archie. "Let's wait until tomorrow evening. I'm gonna be wiped in the morning."

"Okay, okay. Take me home and we'll pick this up tomorrow evening."

Tomorrow Evening: Online!

The next evening, they sat at their computer. It was nothing fancy, just a regular computer bought at the local department store. They had a modem hooked up to it, too, which didn't cost too much. They also had a program that came with the modem that let them call up different computer systems.

So they had their computer, their modem, and the software that came with the modem, called a terminal program. They told the program to dial the number listed in the advertisement. This process could be different for different computers and different terminal programs.

A dial tone sounded, followed by a ring. A tiny little voice came through the speaker on the modem.

"Hello? Hello? HELLO!!!"

He pressed (ALT)-(H) to hang up the phone line. The voice stopped.

"Oops," laughed Archie. "I typed in the wrong phone number. I wonder . . . oh my gosh, that was the home phone number of the boss at our day job! Hope he doesn't have . . ."

The phone rang.

"Call return," added Veronica.

"Don't answer it," said Archie, laughing. He jumped out of his chair and ran to the answering machine and unplugged it. The ringing eventually stopped. He laughed and said, "Let's try that again."

This time he typed in the proper number, and the little speaker on the modem made a highpitched whine and static sounds. Finally, a message appeared on the screen:

> **Welcome to Simple Internet Connection,**
> **your simple connection to the Internet!**
> **Please log in or type newuser.**
> **login:**

"I guess we type 'newuser'?" said Archie.

"Yeah," said Veronica. "It should give us what's known as a login name and password. The login name is just a name we'd like the computer world to know us by, and the password is a secret word we type in to access the computer."

Archie typed **newuser** and pressed (ENTER). Another message appeared:

> **Welcome new user!**
> **Please enter your real name, a name you'd like to use for your**
> **account, and a password.**
> **Real name:**

Archie typed his real name, then stopped. "A name for our account? Do they mean a name we'll use that'll be our Internet address?"

"Yup, at least that'll be the first part of our Internet address. We'll also use that name next time we log in, after the login prompt. I guess it doesn't have to be our real name. Some computers you log into require your real name, but I guess this one doesn't, since it didn't say so. So it can be pretty much anything. What do you think it should it be?"

"How about Galileo, one of my favorite scientists?" said Archie.

"That's fine."

Archie typed

galileo

and pressed (ENTER). "Password . . . hmm . . . maybe my first name?"

"No, that would be too obvious," said Veronica. "It should be something we can remember, but not something someone else is likely to figure out. On some computers that you log into, you'll be warned that the password must consist of both letters and numbers. But this computer doesn't seem to mind if it's all let-ters, or all numbers."

"What's the password for?" asked Archie.

"It's to keep other people from logging into the computer as you and doing things they're not supposed to, such as sending email to others while pretending to be you."

"That makes sense. How about kepler for the password?"

"kepler? That's fine."

Archie typed **kepler** for his password. "Uh, it's a little known fact that, uh, Kepler was another great scientist. Discovered some laws about the planets. You see, he wasn't respected . . ."

"Yeah, I think I learned about him in school. I'd rather forget about that stuff."

"There," said Archie. "We're online. It never asked for a credit card number."

"Maybe it will later. If not, then I guess it's free. I thought the ad said it cost money, but maybe they're having a special or something. Now. How to get to the email stuff. Looks like we have a menu."

"A menu?"

"Yeah, a list of items to choose from. Look at this. It's the main menu."

> **Main Menu**
> a. **Mail**
> b. **Usenet News**
> c. **Unix Shell**
> **Type a letter and press ENTER!**

"Now, other systems will be different, but this one is typical. See, one of the choices is Mail. We can choose that one. Or we can choose the one called Unix shell, and then type the word 'mail'. But just choosing the Mail menu item is easier."

"What was that you said about a shell?"

"I said *Unix shell*. That's basically like a computer where you type a word and press the (ENTER) key to get the computer to do something. In that case we'd just type **mail**."

"Ooh, let's do it that way."

"But just choosing Mail is easier. Of course, on some systems, readers might not get a menu; they might just see a funny little percent symbol, %, which means they're in a shell. So first we'll do the shell, and then the menu. Agreed?"

"Agreed. How'd you get that percent symbol to appear in what you said?"

"Huh?"

"Never mind. Let's do the shell method first. How do I choose an item?"

"Well, the menu item Unix shell has a letter *c* before it, so press the letter (c). Since it's shown as a small *c*, you'd better press a small *c*, not a capital *C*."

"I'll press (c), then." He pressed (c) and the following appeared:

> **This is the Unix shell. Type menu and press Enter to return to the main menu.**
>
> %

"Now what?" said Archie.

"Type **mail** and press (ENTER)."

He did so:

> **%mail**

The screen replied with

> **No mail.**
>
> %

"So? I want to *send* mail!" said Archie. "I hate computers."

"Calm down," said Veronica. "We'll figure it out. Instead, try typing **mail** followed by the address we're sending the mail to."

He typed

> **%mail owner@super.geeks.com**

The computer responded with

> **subject:**

"Type in . . ." said Veronica, ". . . um, **missing**."

Archie typed **missing**, and pressed (ENTER).

> **subject: missing**

He typed the following message:

Hello,

My name is Dr. Archie Finger, Private Investigator. I'm trying to find the owner of Super Geeks, because he disappeared. Please write back.

Thanks!

Veronica said, "I've heard that to complete an email message you type a period on a line all by itself then press (ENTER)."

So that's what Archie did:

.

The computer responded with a % prompt:

%

"I guess it sent out the mail message," said Archie. So what exactly does the percent % sign mean? And see, I even put the symbol in my words, just like you did."

Veronica laughed and said, "The percent is just a *prompt*. That means it's ready for you to type the next command, like **mail**."

"But why the percent? Why not a message like 'type something'?"

"I have no idea. I guess it's just the way Unix computers do it. You know, some computers let you type things in, while some computers let you move a mouse around and point to things. The Macintosh, for instance, lets you use a mouse. And on DOS computers you generally have to type in what you want and press (ENTER) when you're finished. Well, Unix seems to be the same way. The percent symbol just sort of means 'type something,' as you put it."

"Okay," said Archie. "Let's do the menu version of the mail now." He typed **menu** and pressed (ENTER). The main menu appeared again.

"Remember," said Veronica, "not all computers will have a menu version, while others may have only a menu. And if they have both, the way to go from the shell to the menu may not be the same as here. What I mean is, typing **menu** may not work on all computers. When it doesn't, the computer should give you instructions, as it did here."

"Now," said Archie, "let's do the menu version of mail." He pressed the (A) key to choose the first item in the menu, Mail. The following appeared:

Welcome to the Menu version of the Electronic Mail System!
Your direct link to the Internet! Your Internet address is . . .

galileo@simple.int.com

Send To:

"I guess that's gonna be our Internet address," said Archie. "So when people somewhere else want to send *us* a message, they type that in. It looks similar to the email address we have for our missing person."

"Yeah. The first word is usually the login name on the computer, just like galileo is for us. Then there's usually an @, followed by the registered computer name. Generally the computer name has some words separated by periods. The end is often the word 'com,' which stands for commercial. Sometimes they'll end in 'edu,' which means educational institution. By the way, the period is pronounced 'dot,' and the @ is pronounced 'at.' So our address is pronounced, 'galileo at simple dot int dot com.'"

"Now," said Archie, "I'll type the same name as before."

Send To: owner@super.geeks.com

The following appeared:

Subject:

"And the same subject," he said.

Subject: Missing

"Guess I'll type the same message." He typed **Missing** again and pressed (ENTER). The following appeared:

Enter your message below. Type a single period on a blank line to send your message out into the great wide Internet!

He typed the following:

Hello,

My name is Dr. Archie Finger, Private Investigator. I'm trying to find the owner of Super Geeks, because he disappeared. Please write back.

Thanks!

    .

Archie made sure he typed a period on the last line, all by itself. There was a short delay and the following message appeared:

Your message has been sent. Note that it could be a couple hours or even a couple days before the message arrives at its destination.

The main menu appeared again.

"Pretty cool," said Archie. "It looks like the menu version gives you a lot more instructions as you go."

"Yeah, that's often the case. We'd better log out now."

"How do I do that?"

"Just type **logout**."

"Log out?"

"Yeah, like this." She typed at the computer:

logout

"There," she said. "Done. We're no longer connected." She pressed (ALT)-(H), which, for the terminal program they were using, happened to be the way to disconnect the phone line. For other programs, this process may be different.

"Pretty wild," said Archie.

"Pretty wild," agreed Veronica. "Let's call it a day. You up for another bagel?"

"Sure."

They headed for the 24-hour bagel shop to pick up a couple of bagels.

CHAPTER 2
A Million and One Messages

A Million and One Messages

It was six o'clock in the evening, and Archie was stuck in traffic as he tried to drive home from his day job at the accounting firm. Slowly, slowly the cars drifted forward, then stopped, then drifted forward.

Archie glanced down at the gas gauge and noticed it was getting a bit low. There was a gas station ahead; eventually when he reached it he'd pull in.

After a few minutes he finally approached the gas station. He turned in and pulled up to a pump. Climbing out of his car, he noticed two people standing outside their car beside another pump. He thought he heard the word "Internet" come out of one of their mouths.

He strained to listen. They were definitely talking about the Internet. One of them referred to it as the "information highway." Archie had heard that term before, but hadn't put it together with the Internet.

Then he heard something strange come from one of the two people. It sounded sort of like "Soash dot penpals." Then as they were talking, the other person said the same thing. "I was in soash dot penpals and saw a posting by a rock musician looking to exchange email with other rock musicians."

Archie considered that. The word "penpals" would make sense, since they're talking about exchanging email. But what was that thing that sounded like "soash dot?"

He finished pumping his gas, went over and paid for it, and returned to his car. Once on the road again, stuck in traffic, he began thinking about the Internet mystery and finding the missing person. It was just yesterday he and Veronica were at the person's house and he discovered the Internet.

But today the boss at the firm sent Veronica out of town on business. What a bummer. Looks like Archie's on his own for this one. She's not due back for a whole week. And missing people aren't supposed to stay missing for that long.

Archie then began thinking about the conversation he overheard at the gas station. "Soash dot penpals." The words rang through his mind. What could that possibly mean?

Discovering Usenet

It was now late in the evening, and Archie was staring at the computer screen. His eyes felt like they would fall out of his head at any moment.

Once again he looked at the email message from the night before:

> Thanks for responding. I knew you'd find the address. Now play with Usenet for a while and get back with me. And see if you can find the secret board.

Usenet, usenet. That's something to do with network news. Archie had figured out what network news was. Partly from just playing with it; partly from reading the *Everything* book. *Everything* gave a rather drawn-out, long-winded explanation, but still Archie was able to figure a lot out from it.

He figured out that Usenet was basically a gigantic group of discussion topics, and people exchanged messages, called articles, over the Internet relating to these topics. It's a lot like email, with one big catch: When somebody sends out an article in a topic, it goes out to almost everyone, unlike email, which goes to a particular user only.

Thousands and thousands of people each day post articles in the various groups, and these articles get copied automatically from computer to computer until nearly every computer on the Internet has a copy. It's like sending email to everyone. If one person posts an article in a particular discussion group, that article winds up on almost every computer on the Internet, for every person to see. And people can post responses, which in turn go to every other computer.

Archie felt a little overwhelmed at this idea, but was glad to see Usenet is divided into several major groups of discussion topics, and each of these major groups is divided into smaller, more specific topics. And many of these topics are broken up even further.

You don't have to read articles posted in every discussion group. You need only see the topics you want to see.

The groups are called newsgroups and have names like comp.graphics and rec.humor and sci.math.research and alt.music.makers and alt.books.reviews and soc.penpals.

Archie now knew what those people at the gas station were talking about—soc.penpals, pronounced, "soash dot penpals."

Each group name is composed of two or more words separated by periods. The first word is the major group. The second word is the more specific topic; and the words that follow, if there are any, are even more specific.

For instance, in sci.math.research, the topic is in the major group sci, meaning science. The specific topic is math, and even more specifically, the discussions are about research in the field of mathematics.

So, thought Archie, if one person posts an article in the soc.penpals group, it will get copied to thousands of computers, and everyone who reads the soc.penpals group will see the article. Archie realized that Usenet news is sort of like a party line for email. For each discussion group, thousands of articles move around the Internet from computer to computer, and when one person posts an article, it's for everyone in the discussion group to see.

The *Everything* book then went on to explain that within these discussion groups there are individual subjects. It said that each posting has a subject line, just as regular email does. This helps you know which postings you want to read and which to skip.

Reading the News

When Archie logged onto his system, he was unaware of all the news. There was no message telling him he received news, or anything. But he discovered it was most certainly there. Tons of news, in fact.

To read it, the *Everything* book told him to type a strange couple of letters, in the same way he had to type **mail** to read his mail. The letters were

>nn

and had to be typed in lowercase. Apparently the two letters stood for "No News," which was short for "No News is Good News, but nn is better." Pretty bizarre, thought Archie. But, I can pretend that nn stands for netnews.

After he typed **nn**, the screen looked like this:

	Newsgroup: alt.music.makers			
a	John Lennon	669		BEATLES FAQ:Best Beatles songs ever
b	Jim Morrison	909		New poetry newsgroups
c	Jim Morrison	777		FAQ: Poetry and Lyrics
d	Buddy Holly	363		Music FAQ: Life of Buddy Holly
e	Jimi Hendrix	661	[2]	Playing the guitar
f	Buddy Holly	541		Life on the road
g	Jack Benny	950		Looking for violin manufacturer
h	John Lennon	591		Has anyone seen Paul lately?
— 02:35 — SELECT — help:? ——-Top 8%——-				

Archie wasn't sure what to do next. He looked at the *Everything* book. Fortunately, it did a pretty good job of explaining things. It started with a warning though:

> *Warning:* The nn news reader is not easy to use. If your system offers another news reader instead of nn, such as trn, you'll probably do better with the other. If you don't have access to anything but nn, be ready for some frustration. But be patient; eventually you'll get the feel. If you do have access to something other than nn, you may still want to read the following to get a general feel for how news readers work.
>
> One question is, how do you know if your system has a better reader? Chances are, when you log on, there will be a message telling you what news reader to use. If there isn't, you can send email to the sysop of the system, whose name should appear when you log in, or

when you originally signed up and were given instructions for using the system.

Archie didn't see anything on his screen that suggested there was a better news reader, so he decided he'd try and use nn. However, he knew that if there was another news reader, he'd take the *Everything* book's advice.

He read on:

There are two things to keep in mind when reading news with the nn news reader. First is that the (SPACEBAR) is your friend. Second, the (?) key is your second-best friend.

There are two things you do in nn. First, you choose which articles you want to read. (This is called selection mode.) Second, you read those articles. (This is called reading mode.)

Selection Mode

To choose articles, you work in what's known as selection mode. Your screen will look something like the previous screen.

To pick the articles you want to read, press the lowercase letter in the far left column. For instance, to read the message called "Looking for violin manufacturer," press lowercase (G). A * will appear next to the letter, as in the following text, meaning you'll go back to it after you've picked all the articles you want to read.

```
              Newsgroup: alt.music.makers
   a  John Lennon    669        BEATLES FAQ:Best Beatles songs ever
   b  Jim Morrison   909        New poetry newsgroups
   c  Jim Morrison   777        FAQ: Poetry and Lyrics
   d  Buddy Holly    363        Music FAQ: Life of Buddy Holly
   e  Jimi Hendrix   661  [2]   Playing the guitar
   f  Buddy Holly    541        Life on the road
  *g  Jack Benny     950        Looking for violin manufacturer
   h  John Lennon    591        Has anyone seen Paul lately?
  — 02:35 — SELECT — help:? ——-Top 8%——
```

When you've picked all the articles on that screen to read, press (SPACEBAR). Another screen of article subjects may appear, just like the last; or, if there are no more articles, the individual articles you've chosen will show up on the screen. Remember, there are two modes: selection mode and reading mode.

The key idea here is that you hit (SPACEBAR) over and over to go from screen to screen, while choosing articles in each screen as they appear by pressing the lowercase letters. When you're on the last page of selections, hitting (SPACEBAR) yet again brings up the actual articles you've selected, as shown in the following text. You're now in reading mode.

Jack Benny   Fri, 18 Mar 1994 01:20

Hello everyone!

I'm looking for the address of any violin manufacturers that may be in Southern California.

Please email responses to
jack@benny.com
Thanks!

```
-        Jack Benny        -
-        Comedian         -
```

— 02:36 —alt.music.makers— LAST —help:?—Top 0%—

Reading Mode

Once in reading mode, your screen will have an article on it. At the top will be the name of the person who posted the article, along with the date and time the article was posted. You can read the article and press (SPACEBAR) to go to the next page. The next page will either be more of the same article, if it's long, or the next article.

Hit (SPACEBAR) again and again to move from screen to screen of articles. When you're at the end of the last article, pressing (SPACEBAR) yet again takes you back to selection mode.

Again, the key idea here is pressing (SPACEBAR) over and over.

The Incredible Space, Space, Spacebar

Let's review this, thought Archie. When I'm in selection mode, I'll see a screen of article subjects. I choose the articles I want to read by pressing the lowercase letters shown in the left side. Then I hit (SPACEBAR) to go to the next page of article subjects. And I do the same thing, pressing (SPACEBAR) to go from page to page.

When I'm on the last page, I press (SPACEBAR) yet again. That takes me to the actual articles, in reading mode.

Then, once in reading mode, I hit (SPACEBAR) again and again to move from article to article. When I'm at the last article, I hit (SPACEBAR) yet again to get back to selection mode.

That's not so bad, thought Archie. I think I can handle that!

One thing to realize, the *Everything* book pointed out, is that for each article subject there may be more than one article. So even if you only pick one subject, you may get more than one article.

Archie had also noticed something that he was able to figure out for himself. At the bottom of the selection screen was a little number with a percent symbol, such as 10%. This told how far he was through the selection screens. That gave him an idea of how far he had to go before getting to the last page.

One More Time

Archie had to step back from the computer for a moment and put everything together. So, thought Archie, this nn news reader is for reading network news, which thousands of people post every day. The news is divided into lots of discussion groups, and each news article has a subject line.

When I run nn, thought Archie, the first thing I see is a list of subjects. I can choose which ones I want to read, and then I can press (SPACEBAR) to see another page of subjects. I can press (SPACEBAR) over and over until I get to the last page of subjects. After that the actual articles I've chosen will appear.

But Wait, There Are More Ways to Move Around

Already, though, Archie had a few questions. First, what if he wants to back up a page?

The *Everything* book had a section called "There's Much More." Archie just skimmed over it; he didn't want to learn every little detail about nn, only the basics. Once he was familiar with using it, he could delve deeper. But for now, thought Archie, I'll stick to the simple stuff.

To back up a page while in selection mode, Archie discovered, you press the (<) key, since that points to the left, sort of like pointing to the previous page.

The *Everything* book added that if you want to jump right to reading mode without spacing through all the following pages of article subjects, press (SHIFT)-(Z). That way, you can read things on a per-message basis: Pick an article by pressing its lowercase letter, then press (SHIFT)-(Z) to read it.

That's not too tough.

🖈 Press (SPACEBAR) for the next page, then again and again until you're at the end.

🖈 Press (<) for the previous page.

🖈 Press (SHIFT)-(Z) to read, or, if on the last page, just press (SPACEBAR) yet again.

In reading mode, there are a few ways to move around. To back up a page, press the (P) key, for the previous page. To get out of reading mode, press (SPACEBAR), if on the last page, or (=) from any page.

I think I can handle that, too, thought Archie.

🖈 Press (SPACEBAR) for next page, then again and again until you're through all articles.

🖈 Press (BACKSPACE) for the previous page (Mac users can use (DELETE)).

🖈 Press (N) to go to the next article.

🖈 Press (P) for the previous article.

🖈 Press (=) to get back to selection mode.

Archie figured that the more he used the reader, the more he'd become familiar with these keys.

Moving Between Groups

Archie read in the *Everything* book that there was another way of getting around in selection mode: moving between message groups.

Currently, Archie was in rec.music.makers. But what if he wanted to go to a different group, such as rec.books.reviews?

The *Everything* book explained that to "go" to a group, you press (SHIFT)-(G). Archie did, and saw the following:

Group or Folder:

He typed

rec.music.makers

and pressed (ENTER). There was a pause, and soon the screen filled again with a bunch of article subjects:

Newsgroup: alt.books.reviews

a	E. Hemmingway	669	**Writing Workshop Starting!**
b	Agatha Christie	909	**Anyone read The Kidnapped Prime Minister?**
c	Scott Fitgerald	777	**Review of Fall of the House of Usher**
d	Agatha Christie	125	**Just finished 2010 and loved it!**
e	HG Wells	661	**Has anyone read To Build a Fire?**
f	Edgar Poe	541	**Looking for ten books to read this spring**
g	Edgar Poe	950 [2]	**Need a good book on C++ programming**
h	Jack London	591	**Online Writers group forming**
i	Nate Hawthorne	994	**Where is the FAQ?**

— 02:35 — SELECT — help:? ——Top 8%——

The *Everything* book had an interesting note, though. Once you press (SHIFT)-(G) to go to a newsgroup, you can press (SHIFT)-(P) to go back to the previous news-group. Then press (SHIFT)-(N) to go to the next one—the same one you pressed (SHIFT)-(G) to get to, before. (SHIFT)-(P) to go to the previous; (SHIFT)-(N) to go to the next. The book added that once you've pressed (SHIFT)-(G) to get to a newsgroup, and you later move to another, you have to press (SHIFT)-(P) or (SHIFT)-(N) to move around and get to the one you pressed (SHIFT)-(G) for previously, until you leave nn and return later.

I've Read the Articles, Now What?

Archie knew that he was just like all the other people on the Internet, and there was no reason he couldn't post an article. But he was a little nervous. There were thousands and thousands of people out there that may read the article.

Archie decided there were probably certain rules he should abide by; but for now he'd just remember that if he decided to post an article, he'd be polite, and not swear. Later, in Chapter 9, he'll look more closely at all the rules about posting.

He still wasn't sure he wanted to post, but he decided to at least read up on how to do it.

The *Everything* book stated that if you're reading an article and wish to reply to it—that is, send a follow-up article for everyone to see—press (F) for follow-up. You will then be presented with what's called an editor, where you can type and edit an article for everyone to see. Or, to post an article with a brand new subject—not a follow-up to someone else's—type a ⊙ (colon), type **post**, and then press (ENTER). Just like posting a follow-up, you will be given an editor to type your article in.

The *Everything* book had another warning:

> *Warning:* Just like nn, the typical editor, called vi (pronounced either "vie" or "vee-eye") is a pain to use. If you have an alternate, use it. Also, if you want to practice posting articles, try the misc.test group.

Archie had no idea, but supposed he'd probably be lucky enough to be stuck with the vi editor.

He decided to try posting his own article, but decided to do it from the misc.test group.

He typed (SHIFT)-(G) and waited a moment, and when asked

Group or Folder:

he typed

misc.test.

and pressed (ENTER).

The screen then was in selection mode, showing a set of message lines for the group misc.test.

By the *Everything* book's instructions, Archie then typed

:post

(including the colon) and pressed (ENTER).

He saw the following:

POST to group

He typed

misc.test

and pressed (ENTER). He then saw

Subject:

He typed

Test of a post!

and pressed (ENTER). Next he saw

Keywords

He wasn't sure what that meant. He figured it must be if someone does some sort of search or something, that's what they can find this posting under. So he typed

test

and pressed (ENTER). He figured it really didn't matter a whole lot what he typed there. He then saw

Distribution: (default 'world')

and he just pressed (ENTER). He wanted the whole world to see this article—or, at least, everyone on the planet who gets the misc.test newsgroup.

He then saw the thing called vi:

```
~
~
~
~
~
~
~
~
~
~
"/tmp/ab76246" 0 lines, 0 characters
```

Archie thought to himself, boy, this looks like it's gonna be fun.

The *Everything* book said that like the nn news reader, the vi editor has two modes. Only in this case those modes are command mode and edit mode.

In edit mode, you can type in your article.

In command mode, you can do things like delete a word from your article, move the cursor around to different places, and finish editing the article.

The *Everything* book had a whole bunch of notes on the editor; Archie only read what seemed important. He found that the editor starts up in command mode, and to go to edit mode to begin typing his article, he should press the small (i) key (*i* stands for insert text). He did so, and didn't see anything all that different. Then he started typing:

Hello, this is a test

and this is what he saw on his screen:

```
Hello, this is a test
~
~
~
~
~
~
~
~
"/tmp/ab76246" 0 lines, 0 characters
```

Then, to go back to command mode, Archie pressed (ESC). Again he didn't really see much of anything that was different.

The book said to type a (:) (colon), followed by (w) and then (ENTER) to save the message. Archie did so.

He then saw the following:

a)bort e)dit h)old m)ail r)eedit s)end v)iew w)rite

Action: (post article)

He just pressed ⟨ENTER⟩ since what he wanted to do, post the article, was already written there for him.

He felt a little nervous that the article he typed just went out to everybody. Would everyone read it? He wasn't sure. He tried not to worry too much about it, but couldn't help worrying just a little.

A Friendly Face

Archie spent some time reading articles, and he saw some strange stuff. Occasionally he'd come across a colon, followed by a minus sign, followed by a right parenthesis, like this:

> :-)

He looked at it sideways and realized it was a silly little smiley face. Okay, that's cute, thought Archie. Apparently people were putting that in their articles to mean things like, "That was just a joke," or "Don't worry I'm not angry," or whatever, depending on the particular article. He also saw not-so-smiley faces to indicate other emotions. A couple of the more common ones were:

> :-(
> :-0

He also saw lots of acronyms. He was able to figure most of them out, but a couple he had to look up in the *Everything* book. Here are some of them:

IMHO stands for in my humble opinion or in my honest opinion.

BTW stands for by the way.

ROFL stands for rolling on the floor laughing.

OTOH stands for on the other hand.

RTFM stands for read the friendly manual. The *F* could stand for some other adjectives, too.

LOL stands for laughing out loud.

With that, Archie called it a day.

CHAPTER 3

Where, What, When?

Archie was typing at his computer, when his fingers started to ache. "Enough of this," he said, standing up and walking away from the computer. He went upstairs and sat down in the living room and turned on the TV. He gazed at the TV, but his mind was elsewhere. There was something about the computer and the Internet that was bothering him.

It was as if messages were moving from computer to computer, but something wasn't quite right. When he logged onto the Simple Internet Connection, he was watching Usenet messages move across the screen on his own computer. But were those messages actually being stored on his own computer? If not, where were they?

Then there was the issue of programs running. He would type **mail** to run the mail-reader program, but that didn't completely make sense. When he wants to run a program on his own computer, such as his word processor, it's running on the computer sitting on the floor by his desk, and the monitor that shows everything is hooked up to that computer. But when he's logged into the Simple Internet computer, and he types **mail** to run the mail-reader program, where is it running?

Archie figured that when he types **mail**, he's telling the Simple Internet computer to run the mail program, and the Simple Internet computer is somehow sending stuff over the phone lines to appear on the screen of Archie's computer. But Archie wasn't completely positive about this, so he decided to look it up in the *Everything* book.

He stood up and went back downstairs. He looked around the room for the *Everything* book. He spotted it on the floor next to his desk, which was his favorite spot for keeping all his notes and books. He picked it up and began paging through it when a small sheet of paper fell out. It was Veronica's handwriting. She had written

If you're getting confused, I made a videotape that you can watch. The tape is upstairs by your VCR.

"Cool," he said. He headed upstairs, found the tape, threw it into the VCR, and started it rolling.

Veronica appeared on the TV screen. "Hi, Archie. Glad you decided to watch this tape. I thought I'd better leave you with some last-minute information explaining some of this stuff about where mail messages are and how programs run. Let's first talk about something called a file."

Files and Directories

"A *file*," said Veronica, "is a set of information usually stored on a disk. That disk can be a floppy disk that you shove into the computer, or it can be a fixed disk inside the computer, usually called a hard disk or hard drive.

"A file holds information. For instance, when you use a word processor to write a letter to the editors of the newspaper, you can print it on a sheet of paper and mail it, and you can also save the information on a disk. The piece of information on disk is a file. You can use the computer to copy the file from one disk to another, or make a duplicate file, or delete it. Here's Figure 3-1." A picture appeared on the screen that looked like Figure 3-1.

"Notice the file is saved inside the computer on the hard drive," said Veronica. "Most disks, whether floppy or hard, can hold lots of files. Hard drives usually hold far more than the floppies, though. But with all those files, you need a way to organize them. So the designers of the computer put together a method for organizing them. It's a hierarchy of groups of files called a *directory* system. Basically it works like this: The disk gets divided into several areas called directories. These directories are sort of like folders containing other folders or documents. Take a look at Figure 3-2."

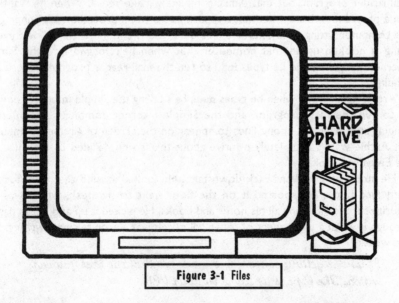

Figure 3-1 Files

"That makes sense," said Archie. "This directory is where we store files. But wouldn't it get messy, having all those files crammed in there?"

Amazingly, Veronica responded, even though she was on videotape. "You can store all your files in this one directory, but that could get messy. So instead, you can break this main directory up into subdirectories. See Figure 3-3. Notice we have two subdirectories, one for Letters to Editors, and one for Letters to Politicians. You could have other subdirectories, too, depending on what you store on your computer.

"The interesting thing is that you can still store files in the main directory. So really we have a total of three directories here: the first, and two subdirectories. Let's draw it like Figure 3-4. Notice our main directory holds everything else, just like a filing cabinet. For some reason when the inventors of the computer put together this directory concept, they called the main directory the *root* directory. The main or top directory is called the root, and the others are its subdirectories.

"Remember," continued Veronica, "these directories are simply ways of organizing files on your disk and keeping track of them. Here we have the main directory that holds the subdirectories, and we have two subdirectories, one to hold letters to editors, and one to hold letters to politicians. We could also put files in the root directory, if we want. We can put files into any directory or subdirectory."

Archie asked her, "But what if we don't want to write any letters to politicians?"

"Good question," said Veronica. "We can organize our disks however we want. If we don't want to write any letters at all, then we don't need either of these two subdirectories. But we might have other subdirectories such as Tax

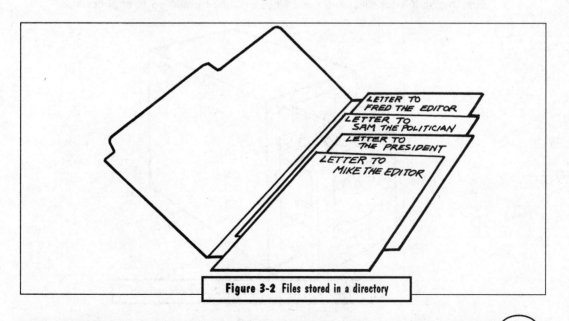

Figure 3-2 Files stored in a directory

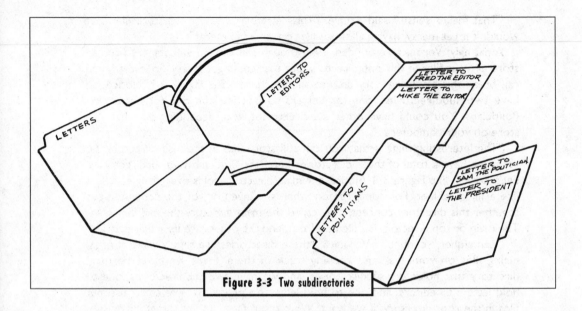

Figure 3-3 Two subdirectories

Forms or Bank Information or whatever. These subdirectories might be used by our accounting programs. Does that make sense?"

"Sort of. Can you explain it again?" asked Archie.

"Sure. We can organize our hard drive in pretty much any way we see fit. We can break the root directory into any set of subdirectories, depending on how we want to organize our files. And these files can come from all sorts of places, such

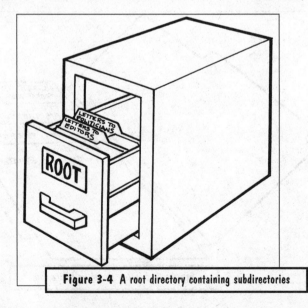

Figure 3-4 A root directory containing subdirectories

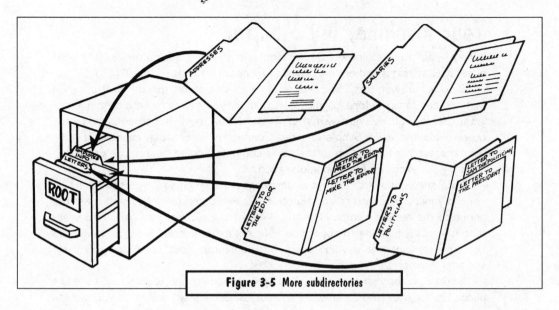

Figure 3-5 More subdirectories

as when we write a letter in our word processor and save it to disk, or if we're using our accounting program and need to save data to disk. Or if we're using our company program that keeps track of employee information and we need to save the employee information to disk."

"Wait a minute," Archie said. "What if we're using one of those programs and we don't save the information to disk?"

"Then it'll get lost when we shut the computer off. That's the whole idea behind having disks. To save the information so it doesn't go away when we kill the power."

"So let's see if I have all this straight," said Archie. "We can enter something into our computer, and then save it as a file on a disk. And we can organize those files into a directory tree, keeping them nice and neat. Right?"

"That's right. And there's more. We can take those subdirectories and make even more subdirectories under those. So let's start over and say that we have our root directory, with two subdirectories. One is for letters, one is for employee information."

Veronica continued, "Now let's break those subdirectories into subdirectories of their own. For Letters, let's have To Editors and To Politicians. For Employee Info, let's have Addresses and Salaries. Let's list some sample files, too. Look at Figure 3-5."

Veronica said, "Incidentally, often people say 'directory' to mean either directory or subdirectory. Just a little timesaving thing. Also, remember that we can store files in any of these directories, not just the bottom ones. There can even be files in the root directory."

Your Machine, My Monitor

"Okay," said Archie, "now I understand about files and directories. But what about mail messages and Usenet news? How does that relate to this?"

"Before I answer that," said Veronica, "let's talk about the terminal program that you had to use before logging in. Remember you had to run the terminal program that let you dial out with your modem. You used that to connect to the other computer at the Simple Internet Connection. When that happens, it's like your computer is hooked up to the other computer, called the remote computer, and they can exchange files and information.

"But," she continued, "it's not as simple as that. When you type something on your keyboard, the letters and numbers (called characters) get sent over the phone to the remote computer. And it keeps track of what you type. And every time it wants something to appear on your computer screen, it sends the letters and numbers out over the phone to your computer. Your computer gets them and puts them on the screen.

"So let's go through that again. You type something and it gets sent over the phone line for the remote computer to process. Everything you see on your screen came over the phone lines from the other computer. Check out Figure 3-6.

"Really," she said, "the terminal program mainly sends letters and numbers, called characters, to the remote computer, and when it receives characters back from the remote computer, it displays them on the screen."

"But wait," Archie said. "When I type something, such as an email message, the actual letters I type are appearing on my own screen. So when I type something, isn't it being sent both to the other computer over the phone, as well as to my own screen?"

"No," said Veronica. "When you type an email message, for instance, the letters you type get sent out over the phone line, and the remote computer receives them for processing. The remote computer then sends them *back* to your computer. And remember, when your computer receives characters, it prints them on the screen. So as you type your email message, the characters you type get sent out over the phone lines, and the remote computer sends them right back, in addition to saving them for processing. When your computer gets them back, that's when they're printed on your screen. The remote computer 'echos' them back to you.

Archie thought about this and something occurred to him. When he types his password when logging in, it doesn't appear on the screen. "So," he said, "when I type a password, it gets sent over the phone lines. But it doesn't appear on the screen because the remote computer isn't echoing it back to me."

"Exactly!" said Veronica. "Let's summarize it. When you type a character, it gets sent to the remote computer. And when your computer receives a character, it puts it on the screen. The remote computer can decide which characters to

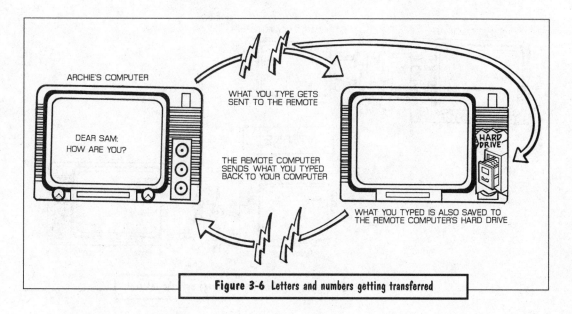

ARCHIE'S COMPUTER

DEAR SAM:
HOW ARE YOU?

WHAT YOU TYPE GETS
SENT TO THE REMOTE

THE REMOTE COMPUTER
SENDS WHAT YOU TYPED
BACK TO YOUR COMPUTER

HARD
DRIVE

WHAT YOU TYPED IS ALSO SAVED TO
THE REMOTE COMPUTER'S HARD DRIVE

Figure 3-6 Letters and numbers getting transferred

echo back and which not to. In the case of passwords, it doesn't echo them back, so they don't appear on your screen. Got it?"

"Sure do!"

"Great! Now let's talk about email messages and Usenet news."

Messages Moving Across the Wire

"Suppose," said Veronica, "you want to compose an email message. You type mail on your computer, and those characters, m-a-i-l get sent over the phone line to the Simple Internet computer. You also type the name of the person you want to send it to. The Simple Internet computer recognizes this sequence of letters, m-a-i-l, as the command for email. It then lets you type in your email message. As you do, each character you type goes out over the phone lines, and the Simple Internet computer remembers exactly what characters you're sending to it. It keeps track of them, and when you're finished, saves it to a file on its own hard drive."

"So I just saved a file on the disk on another computer. Interesting."

"That's right," said Veronica. "You typed the email message, and all your computer did was send each character in the message out over the phone lines as you typed them. The Simple Internet computer caught each one, and built a file on its own disk, and stored those characters in that file. Later on, the mail message will get copied off the Simple Internet computer's disk and sent out over the Internet to the proper computer system."

"So then what happens at the other end?"

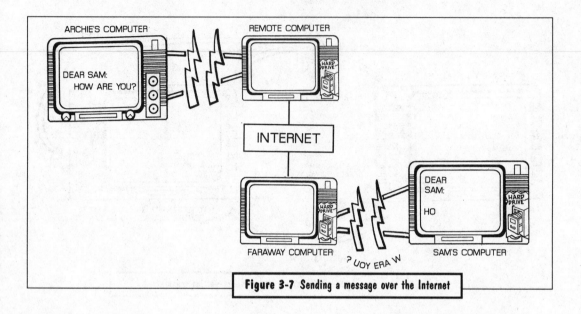

Figure 3-7 Sending a message over the Internet

Veronica said, "The computer that ultimately receives the message will get the data over the Internet, and make a file on its disk, and the mail message will get put inside that file.

"Notice," she added, "the information got sent out over the Internet, and the computer receiving it got the information and saved it as a file on its own disk."

"Is the file still on the Simple Internet computer's disk?"

"Maybe or maybe not. It depends on the particular computer system, and I'm not sure how the Simple Internet computer does it. In most cases, it's not. Once the data is sent out, the computer deletes it from its own disk."

"Now what about the person," said Archie, "who logs into the computer at the other end? What happens then?"

"That person will probably log in to that remote computer, just as you log into the Simple Internet Connection computer. He or she will read the email message by typing mail. That remote computer will send the text over the phone lines to the person's own computer, and the person will see it appear on his or her machine. When the person is done reading it, that remote computer may or may not delete it. Look at Figure 3-7."

She continued, "Whether that remote computer deletes it depends on the system. Most computers will save the incoming mail until the user specifically asks to delete it from the disk. But remember, all this time it's stored on that remote computer's disk, not the user's own disk."

"What if the person wants a copy of the email message on his or her own disk?"

"Then he or she would have to tell the terminal program to do what's called a *capture*: As the mail message is sent over the phone lines for display on his or her screen, the terminal program can also copy the information to a file.

"In other words," said Archie, "as that person's computer receives the characters over the phone line, they get printed on the screen as usual, but also saved to a file."

"That's right. Then later he or she can either print that file or pull it into a word processor or whatever. In fact, generally it's a good idea if you want to save an email message to do it that way—save it to a file on your own machine and maybe print it up—so that it can be deleted from the remote computer's disk. That saves space on the remote computer, and also gives you peace of mind knowing the email message is on your own computer and maybe even printed on paper."

Usenet News

"Okay," said Archie. "That's all making sense. I type an email message, and each character goes to my remote computer that I'm logged into. The remote computer echoes the characters back to my computer, which displays them on the screen. But the remote computer also saves the characters to a file, which gets sent out over the Internet. The computer at the other end receives the data and saves it to a file on its own disk. The user logs in and asks to read the mail, and the characters in the file get sent out over the phone lines onto his or her own computer's screen."

"Exactly," said Veronica. "Now let's talk about Usenet news. That works in much the same way, except when you write a message it goes to almost every computer on the Internet, not just one. And almost every user out there can see it, not just one user. It's much like sending email to everybody."

"Question," said Archie. "The figure says 'pretty much every computer.' That implies not every computer gets the message?"

"That's correct," said Veronica. "That's because not every computer on the Internet gets every Usenet group, that's all. It's up to the owner of that particular computer to decide which Usenet groups to get."

"Can the users delete the messages, in the same way they delete email?"

"No, they can't. The computer usually will store each Usenet news message for a certain amount of time, such as a week or two, and then delete it."

"But what happens when I mark a news message as 'read' when I'm reading news?"

"The computer just makes a note that you read the news item. It doesn't actually delete it."

"That makes sense. After all, if it gets deleted, then other users won't be able to see the message."

"Exactly."

Executing Programs

"The final section of this chapter," said Veronica, "is about programs, not just files. Let's think about what a program is."

"A program?" said Archie. "That's a . . . um . . . gosh, how would you define program?"

"Lots of ways, but let's just say a *program* is something that runs on a computer. Your word processor is a program. Your accounting package is a program. Your terminal program is a program. But how does the computer know how to do the program?" she says.

Archie said, "I have no idea . . . well . . . actually, I guess the program is stored on disk. After all, when you buy those programs, they come on disk and you have to run some sort of annoying installation procedure that seems to set up your computer for it. I guess it copies the program to your hard drive?"

"Generally, yes. The installation stuff copies the program onto your hard drive so it's there, ready for you to run. When you run it, the computer reads the data from the disk into memory, and does what the program tells it to do."

"I have another question," said Archie. "When the program is on the disk, is it a file?"

"Yup. It's stored in a file on the disk. And when it's time to run the program, the computer reads the information out of the file into memory, and it runs the program."

"So why is this all relevant?"

"Because," said Veronica, "we need to understand what's going on when we use the mail reader or the news reader."

"Okay, shoot."

"When you have mail waiting and you type **mail**, those characters in the word 'mail' get sent out over the phone lines, and the remote computer processes them, figuring out that it must run the mail reader. To run the mail reader, it loads the mail program off its own hard drive, and runs that program. That program then lists the mail messages you have. And when it lists them, it sends the characters composing the list out over the phone lines. Your computer receives that information and prints it on the screen. You can request which messages you want to look at by typing the number of the email message. When you do, that number gets sent out over the phone lines, and the mail program gets it, and displays the actual mail message."

"But the point," she added, "is that there's a program running on the other computer. That computer sends stuff out over the phone lines for display on your screen, and you type things on your keyboard telling that remote program what to do next, such as display an email message. It's almost as if your keyboard and screen are hooked up to the remote computer. But keep in mind that there's your own computer and a phone line in between."

"Wow," said Archie. "That's all pretty heavy. I'm gonna get a bagel. Do you want one?"

The tape ended and the VCR stopped.

"Oh, yeah, you're on tape," he said, reaching for a bagel.

CHAPTER 4

The Incredible Robotic Email

Archie felt a bit refreshed after finally learning about files and how they move across the Internet. Things were finally making sense for him, and that was a relief.

Now maybe he could focus his attention on the clue he received a couple days ago. He looked at the copy of the mail message:

> **Get the bitnic list of lists and join the discussion group VPARTY.**
> **Watch for a message about missing people.**

Great. Another perfectly sensible mail message. He looked around the room, wondering if there was another videotape left by Veronica. But he didn't see one.

He heard a door open upstairs. He headed up out of the basement to see who was there. It was Gloria, an elderly lady who came by one evening a week to clean his house for him.

"Hi, Gloria," he said.

"Hi! Whadaya up to?"

"Well, trying to figure out some stuff about lists on the Internet."

"Oh, well, that would have to do with list servers."

"Huh?"

"List servers. They work much like Usenet news, only messages come directly to your email account, just like regular mail messages. And since they get sent to massive amounts of email accounts, they're called mailing lists."

"But . . ."

"You can receive such messages, and they're organized much like Usenet news."

"Umm . . ."

"The way it works is this. You send email to a certain computer system that maintains a mailing list. Your email message then gets forwarded on to everybody on that mailing list. Those people can do the same, and their messages go to everyone on the list. This turns into ongoing discussions.

Using List Servers

"The computer system," she continued, "that maintains this mailing list has a program called a list server, or LISTSERV. Many computers that run LISTSERV maintain more than one mailing list, and each mailing list is dedicated to a certain topic of discussion. Between all the list servers across the country and all their mailing lists, there are over 4,000 mailing lists."

She added, "This whole thing works much like Usenet news, except it all travels over people's mail accounts. And these lists provide several more discussion topics not found in Usenet."

"I see."

"Here's an example. Suppose you're interested in windsurfing, and you find a computer running LISTSERV, and one of the mailing lists this computer maintains is dedicated to discussing windsurfing. You could then send an email message to the list server, asking to be put on the mailing list—you say you wish to subscribe. Each person who subscribes can send out messages for all other subscribers to read. When you send such a message out, it will get emailed to all other subscribers. And since you're a subscriber, you'll get the message, too. But lots and lots of people send out such messages, so you may get an enormous amount of email each day from these people. Let's have a figure." She picked a crayon up off the floor and drew Figure 4-1 on the clean wall.

"And," continued Gloria, "there are lists for almost any topic imaginable. To find out about all the topics, you can have a list of lists automatically emailed to you."

Archie stepped closer and peered into her eyes. "Gloria?"

"Yes, dear?"

"What happened to you?"

"What do you mean?"

"How'd you hear about all this?"

"Well, I'm writing a book on the Internet, and I had to learn all about it before I could write the book."

He was a little confused and just said, "I see . . ."

"I'm hoping to make enough money from the book to start my own maid service."

"Hmm . . ."

"So, any other questions, dear?"

"Umm . . . yeah, actually. Since you know so much about this, you can come downstairs and help me access this list of lists. I want to see what all the discussion topics are."

"Sure. My rates are reasonable."

Archie chuckled. "Come on. Follow me."

They headed downstairs. When they got there, Gloria plopped herself down in front of the computer. It was already on. She began typing like a mad dog. Archie

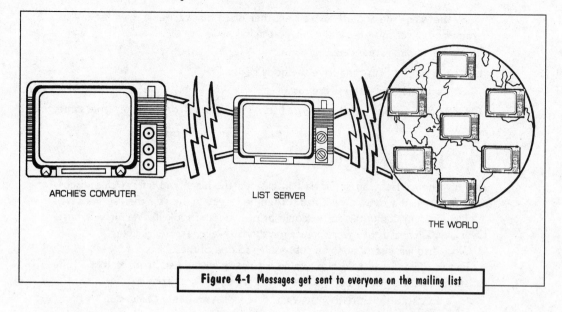

ARCHIE'S COMPUTER   LIST SERVER   THE WORLD

Figure 4-1 Messages get sent to everyone on the mailing list

couldn't keep up watching her. Soon, the terminal program appeared onscreen, and they were logged into the Simple Internet Connection. She clapped her hands. "There. I've logged into your account."

"How'd you get my password?"

"I saw it hanging on the refrigerator door when I came in."

Archie felt embarrassed. "Okay . . ."

"Now," she said. "Let's get the list of lists. There are a couple ways to do this. One way involves a method that we won't see until a later chapter."

Oh, great, thought Archie, another person living life as a book. "Is there a method we already know about?"

"Sure. We'll use regular old email. Basically you just send an email message to a certain place. The computer that receives the email message won't send it to a user; instead it'll see who sent it—you—and send back a gigantic list. The list is huge, but that's okay. That's what this email system is for."

"Who do we send the email to?"

"Well, there are lots and lots of list servers out there, but we can send email to one particular place to get the main list of all the lists."

Gloria typed the following:

> **mail listserv@bitnic.educom.edu**

She left the subject blank. For the body of the letter, she typed

> **list global**

"There," she said. "That's all. Now we just mail it out."

"By the way," she added, "there's another place that carries a main list of lists. If you want to get this one, you can type the following:

mail mail-server@nisc.sri.com

"Leave the subject blank and have the body read

send netinfo/interest-groups

"Or you can do both and get two lists. They should be basically the same, though."

The List of Lists

A couple hours later, after Gloria had cleaned the place and left, Archie discovered the list had arrived over email. When he logged in, he saw the list. He saved it onto his own computer so he could print it up and look it over. It was huge. Over 30,000 lines! There were topics for almost everything imaginable.

Gloria had left instructions on subscribing to one of these lists.

This list, Gloria had told him, would list nearly all the lists from almost all the list servers on the planet. For instance, here are a few lines from it:

ASTRO	ASTRO@GITVM1	Astronomy Discussion List
COMHIST	COMHIST@RPITSVM	History of Human Communication
I-IBMPC	I-IBMPC@UIUCVMD	IBM PC Discussions
MAC-L	MAC-L@YALEVM	Macintosh News and Information
SPORTPSY	SPORTPSY@TEMPLEVM	Exercise and Sports Psychology

Archie figured the address following the @ symbol is the address of the computer running LISTSERV. For example, COMHIST is handled by a list server running on a computer called RPITSVM. Gloria's note said that to send email to these, Archie would have to add .BITNET to the address. So COMHIST is really on the computer called RPITSVM.BITNET.

Archie decided he wanted to learn more about the Macintosh, so he subscribed to the MAC-L list. To do this, he had to send email to the list server running on YALEVM.BITNET:

mail LISTSERV@YALEVM.BITNET

He left the subject line blank. For the main body of the letter, Gloria said to type:

SUB MAC-L Archie Finger

He was told to put SUB, followed by a space, followed by the name of the list he'd like to subscribe to; then another space, his first name, a space, and his last name. This name didn't have to be the same as his login name on the Simple Internet computer; it's what appears on all his messages when he eventually posts some on the mailing list.

Gloria's note had the remark that whatever name you type in is what appears in the return address of the messages you send out to all the subscribers. So be careful, she wrote. Use your real name and don't use somebody else's.

Archie knew it might be an hour or so before he started receiving anything. He figured since the Macintosh is pretty popular, he'd probably receive lots of mail. Perhaps other lists, thought Archie, wouldn't generate much "traffic," and he'd only receive a few messages a day. But even for this list, he'd be patient and give it at least a day or so before he got antsy.

While he was waiting for mail to come, he decided to think a little more about what was happening.

A Plethora of List Servers

Archie reviewed in his mind what he just did. He had sent off for a list of all the mailing lists. These mailing lists are really discussion topics, much like Usenet news. Except with Usenet news, the news items get sent to the Simple Internet computer, or whatever computer the user is logged into, and all the users of that computer can read them. With these mailing lists, which Gloria at one point had called *Bitnet lists,* the individual items get emailed to Archie's own account. Other people who log into the Simple Internet computer can't read the items unless they're also subscribers. In that case, a separate copy will be mailed to them.

So Archie had received the gigantic list of all the mailing lists. These mailing lists are maintained by different computers all across the country. To subscribe to the different mailing lists, Archie needed to send an email message to the actual LISTSERV running on the different computers. In the case above, the Macintosh mailing list is maintained by a computer called YALEVM.BITNET.

Archie wondered how he might eventually have his name removed from the mailing list, but he decided to go to bed and think about it in the morning. "But wait!" he said out loud. "I need to subscribe to the list mentioned in that message I got earlier." He looked at the message again. It said to get the bitnic list of lists, which he had already done, and to join the list called VPARTY.

He figured he could do that. All he had to do was send email to a list server that carried the VPARTY mailing list. But where was that list server?

He looked at the list of lists again, and somewhere towards the end found the line

    **VPARTY   VPARTY@DARTCMS1 VParty, a virtual party with
                                   real people**

He knew what that meant. The VPARTY mailing list is handled by the LISTSERV program running on the computer called DARTCMS1. That meant he had to send an email message to DARTCMS1.BITNET. He typed

    mail LISTSERV@DARTCMS1.BITNET

and, as before, he left the subject line blank. For the body of the message, he typed

SUB VPARTY Archie Finger

and he sent the mail out. He knew that he was sending an email message to the list server at the DARTCMS1 computer, telling it to subscribe him to the mailing list called VPARTY, which was apparently some sort of virtual party, whatever that meant.

A Plethora of Email

The next morning when Archie got up, he logged into the Simple Internet Connection to check his email. There were ten messages. Archie considered this. The night before, he had subscribed to two mailing lists, each handled by list servers on separate computers. Overnight, ten people had sent out messages to be distributed to everyone on the mailing list.

He glanced through the email subjects and found one called

Finding Someone

That was the message he was looking for! He read it

> To everyone seeking a missing person, give up. Someone else who's a better detective will find him. Now for a secret message to the person who's a better detective:
>
> ftp to nerds.r.us and get the ASCII file /pub/secret/findme.txt.

That's a really secret message, thought Archie. I wonder how many other people are on this mailing list who got it?

He looked at the header. The name of the person who sent it was Gloria Strysdale. It was from Gloria, the cleaning lady!

"I have a better way to find the secret person," he mumbled. He grabbed the phone and called Acme Home Cleaning Service.

"Acme," said a nasal voice on the other end. "Can I help you?"

"Yes, can I speak with Gloria Strysdale?"

"I'm sorry, there's nobody here by that name."

"She's one of your cleaning people."

"No sir, I'm afraid not. We have no employees named Gloria."

"Well this is Archie Finger. Can you see who cleaned my place yesterday?"

"One moment."

He could hear the woman typing on a computer.

"I'm sorry, sir, nobody cleaned your place yesterday. The person who was scheduled to clean your home yesterday called in sick, and we were understaffed. So nobody cleaned your place."

"Well somebody was here."

"Don't worry, you won't be billed for the time."

"Does your computer tell who usually cleans my place? Because Gloria comes here every week."

"The usual person is Susan."

"What does she look like?"

"She's a young lady in her early 20s."

"Well that's not Gloria."

"Is there anything else I can help you with?"

"No, that's it." He hung up the phone and wrote down the name Susan.

Archie was feeling a bit suspicious about this whole deal, but at the same time he still had some curiosity about these mailing lists. He decided to wait until the next chapter to continue the mystery, and to figure out what it means to "ftp."

Talking to LISTSERV

To join the mailing lists, Archie had sent email to the respective list servers, one at the computer called DARTCMS1, and one at the computer called YALEVM. The message body simply told the list servers to subscribe him to the mailing lists.

Archie figured that since he had to type **SUB** to subscribe, there was probably a word he could type to unsubscribe, should he decide he didn't want to receive any more of these messages. He also figured there must be a way to post his own messages.

He grabbed the *Everything* book and paged through it. He found the section on LISTSERV.

Canceling a Subscription

The book said that to unsubscribe, you send a message to the LISTSERV computer, just as before, only instead of **SUB**, type **SIGNOFF**. Archie decided to sign off from the VPARTY mailing list, so he typed

    mail **LISTSERV@DARTCMS1.BITNET**

Once again, he left the subject line blank. For the body of the message, he typed

    SIGNOFF VPARTY

The *Everything* book said that this time he didn't need his name; only the name of the mailing list from which he wants to cancel his subscription.

Finding Out About the Lists

Another thing the *Everything* book said Archie could do is ask the list server what lists it carries. Archie already knew about most of the lists; they were in the huge list of lists he got earlier. Still, it might be handy for him to see what lists just a single server carries. For instance, he had seen earlier that there was a list about astronomy, called ASTRO, which was carried by LISTSERV on the computer called GITVM1. Archie had always enjoyed studying astronomy while growing up, and he wondered what other mailing lists this server might carry that would interest him. So instead of rummaging through the giant list of lists for all the mailing lists that are at GITVM1, he could just send email to the actual list server at GITVM1, and ask it personally. To get this information, he typed

    mail **LISTSERV@GITVM1.BITNET**

leaving the subject blank, as usual. He then typed for the body,

LIST

according to instructions in the *Everything* book. He then sent the email on its way.

Getting Help

The *Everything* book said you could also get help from the list server itself. To do this, just send a message as before, but type **HELP** for the body. Archie did that too. The book also said he could combine these things if he wanted to. He could type **LIST** on one line, and **HELP** on the next. Archie decided to try that. First he typed

mail LISTSERV@GITVM1.BITNET

then, for the subject:

LIST
HELP

This, Archie knew, should send him a list of all the mailing lists maintained by this list server, as well as help on how to use the list server. This would all be in one email message, since he's requesting it all from one email message. Of course, he'd also get the list from the previous request, so he'd have two copies of the list. But that's okay.

Archie figured when the help list came, he'd learn even more about talking to LISTSERV. But for now, he knew about these things he could put in the body of his email message:

SUB, followed by the name of a list and a personal name, to subscribe to a particular list handled by this list server.

SIGNOFF, followed by the name of a list, to unsubscribe from a list. (Note that some systems use the word UNSUB instead of SIGNOFF; check the information you receive from HELP to see which command you should use for the particular list server.)

LIST to get a list of all the mailing lists handled by this particular list server.

HELP to get help on how to use the list server. That would include what Archie already knew, such as how to subscribe, but it might have more information, too.

Posting Messages

After reading some of the *Everything* book, Archie figured that LISTSERV is an actual computer program running on some computers, and this program is set up to handle massive amounts of mail. It can receive a mail message and send it out to hundreds or thousands of people, all within a few seconds. And that's how the mailing lists work.

Then, thought Archie, I can do like everyone else on the mailing list and send a message out to go to everyone on the mailing list. The *Everything* book said that to do this, just send email to the name of the mailing list at the computer that handles the list. Archie did just that:

mail MAC-L@YALEVM.BITNET:

subject: I just joined this group

Hello everybody! My name is Archie Finger and I just joined this discussion group! I can't wait to start talking about Mac computers! I also enjoy astronomy, and I'm an accountant by day, a private eye by night!

Archie sent the message out, knowing that all the people on the mailing list would soon receive it.

He noticed it was time to head to work. When he got home, he'd pick up with the mystery again.

CHAPTER 5

Finding The Person

Finding The Person

FTP to the Rescue

Archie picked up the *Everything* book and paged through it. But before he found anything about that thing called FTP, he put the book down.

He looked at the email message again:

ftp to nerds.r.us and get the ASCII file /pub/secret/findme.txt.

It's telling him to do something, like go someplace and get a file. Well, this is the Internet, so that must mean to go someplace electronically, over the modem. Maybe it means log into a computer? No, thought Archie, then it would probably say just that: log into computer such-and-such.

So what does FTP mean?

He picked up the *Everything* book again and dug through it. The index had a single reference to FTP, with some 30 or so pages listed. He went to the first page mentioned. The first sentence said

FTP is used for transferring files. It stands for File Transfer Protocol.

He skipped a few sentences and saw

FTP is a program that you run that establishes a connection to another computer, allowing you to transfer files.

So that's it . . . FTP is a program he runs that lets him hook into another computer and transfer files. And the mail message said to ftp to nerds.r.us and get the file /pub/secret/findme.txt. That makes sense. But why? thought Archie. Why should you have to do this? He then read in the *Everything* book:

Because sometimes another computer may have a file that you want, but you can't directly log into that computer for some reason. For instance, you may not be allowed to directly log in, or you may not *be able to* because it doesn't have a dial-in connection over the phone lines.

That's fine, thought Archie. I probably can't get to this nerds.r.us computer. After all, I don't even know where it is. So how could I get a phone number to log into? It's probably not in the phone book, and the email message certainly didn't include a phone number.

Archie then noticed one more thing in the *Everything* book. It said

Some readers may not have FTP access.

Hmm. That could mean trouble. Better look into that later in this chapter. It also said

Those readers can indirectly use FTP, though, as long as they have email; so they can still read this chapter.

Archie thought, I wonder if I have FTP on my computer?

He looked around the room, ready to see either a videotape or a cleaning lady to save the day and explain a few things to him. But nothing appeared. Looks like I'm on my own for this one, he thought.

Transferring Files with FTP

Let's think this through. This book I'm in is about the Internet, so maybe I have to use my Internet connection.

Hey! Maybe that's it. Maybe the Simple Internet Connection has an FTP program that I can run. Then that computer can do this FTP thing and transfer a file from nerds.r.us to the Simple Internet computer.

I have to remember, though, thought Archie, that this nerds.r.us computer is probably a fake system; it's contrived for this story I'm in. I'd better be sure and include a *real* site at the end of this chapter, so the readers can try FTP, too!

Let's see, thought Archie. I'll log into the Simple Internet Connection, and then do this FTP thing to get the file I need. That'll copy the file from the nerds.r.us computer, across the Internet, and onto the Simple Internet computer. Then I'd have to copy it from the Simple Internet computer to mine. That's not too terribly difficult, because my terminal program has a feature called Download. But I'll worry about that after the file is copied to the Simple Internet computer.

He logged into the Simple Internet Connection. Once on, he typed **ftp** but didn't press the (ENTER) key. He thought for a moment about how with mail he had to type **mail** followed by the address, so that's what he decided to do here. He added

ftp nerds.r.us

To his surprise, after a few moments, something like this appeared on the screen:

Connected to NERDS.R.US

Cool! It's working! I'm connected. But wait a minute . . . let's think about this. Maybe I should draw a diagram of the way I perceive it. He drew Figure 5-1.

Okay, thought Archie, so I'm logged into the Simple Internet computer, and that computer has just connected itself electronically to the computer called nerds.r.us. Hey, I must be catching on to this stuff, since I was able to figure that out!

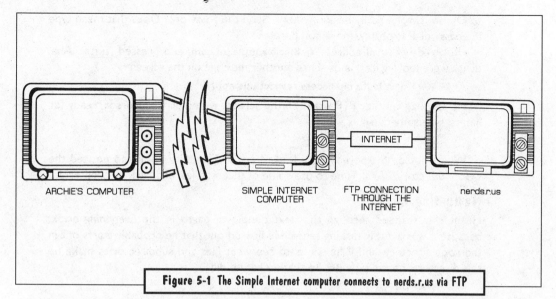

ARCHIE'S COMPUTER

SIMPLE INTERNET
COMPUTER

FTP CONNECTION
THROUGH THE
INTERNET

nerds.r.us

INTERNET

Figure 5-1 The Simple Internet computer connects to nerds.r.us via FTP

He then looked at the computer screen:

220 nerds FTP server (Sun02 4.1) ready.

Name (nerds.r.us:galileo):

Uh-oh. Now what should he do? He looked down at the *Everything* book. Strangely enough, it was becoming more readable. The next section said

When you do anonymous FTP . . .

Waitaminute. Maybe it's not that readable. Anonymous FTP? He read on:

you connect anonymously. That is, you don't have a login account with the computer you're connecting to, so you must log in as an anonymous user. With that login you can look at certain files and get them.

Okay, that sort of makes sense. So I'll log in anonymously without telling the system who I really am. Then I can get the files I need. But how do I do that?

To log in anonymously, you type **anonymous** at the Name prompt.

Aha! Tough one. He ignored most of the junk he saw on the screen, such as the number 220, because he knew it was probably just information for the people who built the computer. He typed **anonymous** at the Name prompt,

Name (nerds.r.us:galileo):anonymous

and pressed (ENTER). The computer responded with

331 Guest login ok, send your complete email address as password.

Oh, so it won't really be anonymous. Send the password? Does that mean type the password? Probably. More computerese.

He typed his email address, **galileo@simple.int.com**, and pressed (ENTER). Aha, things were looking up. He now had another message on the screen:

230 Guest login ok, access restrictions apply.

He also had another FTP word on the screen, with a blinking cursor, ready for him to type something:

ftp>_

What should he type now? He looked at the *Everything* book and noticed the word "directory." Aha! Time to use some of that stuff learned back in Chapter 3.

Navigating in FTP

He quickly scanned through the next couple of pages in the *Everything* book, because it was actually making sense! He figured out that he probably starts out in the root directory, and if he wants to see what files and subdirectories make up this directory, he can type **dir**. So that's what he did:

ftp> dir

The computer responded with more cryptic messages, which he ignored, because they just said something about the connection working. But after that was a list. The screen looked like this:

-rw-rw-r—	1 root	120	1234	May	1	10:50	.message
drwxr-sr-x	2 root	120	512	Jun	2	5:39	pub
drwxr-sr-x	2 root	120	512	Jun	2	5:40	bin
drwxr-sr-x	2 root	120	512	Jun	2	5:41	usr

Figure 5-2 Archie's looking at the root directory

The *Everything* book explained that the first column was a bunch of stuff about the file or directory. If the very first thing in the first column was a *d*, then the entry is a directory. If it's a -, then it's an actual file. The rest of the first column was just gibberish, and Archie ignored it. The last column was the name. So the first line is a file called .message, and the second line is a directory called pub.

Archie figured if he really wanted to learn what all that other stuff meant, he could buy one of those really thick books on the Internet that are supposed to be written for average people and only make you feel below average after you're done reading. The *Everything* book mentioned that this extra stuff that he was skipping had to do with a type of computer called a Unix computer. If he's really brave, maybe in the next lifetime he'd go to the bookstore and buy a book about this thing called Unix. For now, he'll just make sure the book he's living has an entry in the glossary on Unix. And that'll be the end of that.

He noticed the directory called pub. I wonder what's in that directory, he thought. He figured pub must stand for public. He looked in the *Everything* book and found that he could "move" to that directory. Better get a figure. He imagined Figure 5-2, with him looking at the root directory.

To see what's in the pub directory, he has to open that directory. He imagined Figure 5-3.

But how does he go there? He looked in the *Everything* book again and saw that the command to type in is **cd** for change to directory. So that's what he typed in. As with mail and FTP, he typed the place he's going afterwards:

    cd pub

The computer responded with:

    250 CWD command successful.

Figure 5-3 Archie's looking at the pub directory

Well, he didn't type a cwd command, he typed a cd command. Computers are annoying. But at least it says whatever he did was successful.

He then typed **dir** to see if it worked:

    ftp>dir

And it did! He saw the following list, which was definitely different:

-rw-rw-r—	1 root	120	1234	Jun	3	13:20	.message
drwxr-sr-x	2 root	120	512	Jun	3	15:17	fun
drwxr-sr-x	2 root	120	512	Jun	4	5:53	games
drwxr-sr-x	2 root	120	512	Jun	5	4:10	secret

Okay, that's cool. So previously he was in the root directory, and he changed to this other directory called pub. And he's now looking at a listing of the files and directories inside the pub directory.

Archie then noticed an interesting remark in the *Everything* book:

> Some versions of FTP get confused with upper and lowercase, as well as with the slashes in the file names. So sometimes you have to put quotation marks around everything after the command cd, such as **cd "pub"**.

In Archie's case, he was okay; he didn't need the quotation marks, apparently. But he knew he'd better keep that in mind in case he ever logged into a system other than Simple Internet and needed to use FTP.

He looked again at the last directory listing and saw another directory inside this one that he wanted to go to. It was called fun. So he typed

    cd fun

Once again he saw the silly message:

    250 CWD command successful.

He typed

    ftp> dir

and sure enough, he saw yet another listing:

-rw-rw-r—	1 root	120	5234	Jun	4	11:35	FredAge
-rw-rw-r—	1 root	120	2342	Jun	5	9:50	EndWorld
-rw-rw-r—	1 root	120	6547	Jun	10	8:31	eatAtJoes

These files didn't particularly look like much fun. As his mind drifted, a thought suddenly struck him. What if he wanted to get to this directory immediately, without first going through the middle directory, pub? Of course the *Everything* book had an answer, because it has everything he wanted to know. It had something that was confusing, and he only read it once, even though it didn't make sense. It said:

> If you're in the pub directory, you can move to the directory called fun by typing **cd fun**. But if you're somewhere else, you can move directly to the fun directory by typing **cd /pub/fun**, all at once. Note, though, that some versions of FTP have trouble with this, and you

Figure 5-4 A bunch of directories

may need to put the /pub/fun inside quotation marks, for example,
cd "/pub/fun".

Huh? thought Archie. Okay, let's think this through. I'll get a figure going, similar to those in Chapter 3. Here it is, in Figure 5-4.

Suppose, thought Archie, I'm in the directory called root and I want to move to the directory called fun. I can't just type **cd** followed by **fun**, because the *Everything* book says I can't.

"Oh!" Archie shouted. "I see what the book's trying to say!" He wrote a slash, and then the first directory in the root that leads to the directory he's trying to go to—in this case pub. Then he wrote another slash, and wrote the name of the next directory down—in this case fun. He ended up with this:

/pub/fun

So that's how it works. He was catching on. Starting from the right, the fun's parent directory is pub, and pub's parent directory is the root.

Another thought struck him. He'd seen something similar on his PC at work. It worked exactly the same way, except he had to type the backslash at work, \, instead of the forward slash, /. Then there was the guy across the hall who used a Mac and didn't have to worry about any of this stuff at all. But that's okay.

He decided to try it out. He wanted to move to the root directory. He typed **cd** and hesitated. The root doesn't have a name, does it? Oh, wait, for that just do the slash all by itself. So he typed

ftp>cd /

and it responded again with the familiar message about some other command succeeding. He typed **dir** and saw the same stuff he saw earlier when he was in the root. It worked!

Now, he thought, let's go directly to the fun directory, without passing through the pub directory. He typed

> **ftp>cd /pub/fun**

and saw the same success message again. Cool! He did a directory listing, just to be sure he made it there:

> **ftp>dir**
>
> **150 Opening ASCII mode data connection for /bin/ls.**
>
> | | | | | | | | |
> |---|---|---|---|---|---|---|---|
> | -rw-rw-r— | 1 root | 120 | 5234 | Jun | 4 | 11:35 | FredAge |
> | -rw-rw-r— | 1 root | 120 | 2342 | Jun | 5 | 9:50 | EndWorld |
> | -rw-rw-r— | 1 root | 120 | 6547 | Jun | 10 | 8:31 | eatAtJoes |

Sure enough, that's the same directory he saw earlier. Archie was glad he didn't have to put in the stupid quotation marks, but he knew that some systems the readers might be logged into would require them.

Too Much for One Day

Archie was catching on, but at the same time he was starting to feel overwhelmed. He was originally just trying to transfer a file, and now he's thinking about directories. And he's getting into some pretty heavy stuff, too. Far more than he expected. He stepped away from the computer for a moment and took a deep breath. He decided to start a list of everything that's happened. He'll put the final list at the end of the book in an appendix. But what was it he was doing originally? He was trying to transfer a file. And he was using a program called FTP. And then he was learning commands he could type in, once the connection was established. Okay, now he was getting things back in perspective.

Getting the Actual File

Now that Archie understood how to connect and move about in the faraway computer system's directories, he could find the file and get it. He looked again at a sheet of paper where he had copied down the confusing part of the email message. It said to get the "ascii file /pub/secret/findme.txt."

Okay, he understood all the slashes now; that was the full *path name* to get to the file findme.txt. But what was that strange word that started with an *a* and ended with two vowels?

He was getting déjà-vu. He seemed to remember seeing that one before. Oh, yeah, now he remembered. A word processor he used at work had that term in its manuals. Essentially, ASCII meant that the file could be printed on the screen as words for humans to read. And files that weren't of this type usually held other kinds of data, such as pictures that could be drawn on the screen or programs

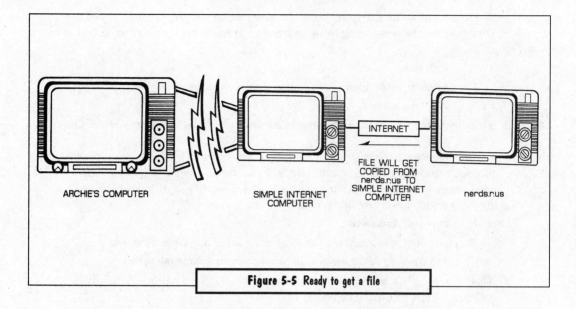

ARCHIE'S COMPUTER

SIMPLE INTERNET COMPUTER

INTERNET

FILE WILL GET COPIED FROM nerds.r.us TO SIMPLE INTERNET COMPUTER

nerds.r.us

Figure 5-5 Ready to get a file

that could be run. He also remembered seeing how to pronounce it: "ask-key." Okay, that was fine. So the file he was getting was an ASCII file. For kicks he'd try and get another file that he didn't need—a file that wasn't ASCII. That way he could learn how to do both.

First things first. He had to find the file. Well, that's easy, because the file's path is right there in the email message. It's /pub/secret. And the file is called findme.txt.

Archie typed

> **ftp>cd /pub/secret**

and pressed (ENTER). After seeing the success message, he typed in

> **ftp>dir**

and saw another list of files and directories:

```
-rw-rw-r—    1 root    120   1234   Jul   5   12:32  readme
-rw-rw-r—    1 root    120   5132   Jul   6   10:54  dontread
-rw-rw-r—    1 root    120   60     Jul   8   6:05   findme.txt
```

And there was the file findme.txt! Now to get it. He wanted to copy it from the faraway computer to the Simple Internet computer. Better get a figure for this. He imagined Figure 5-5.

The file would move from the faraway computer to the Simple Internet computer. Then he'd use his terminal program to pull it down off the Simple Internet computer to his own. Okay, that's fair.

But how to do that?

He glanced at the *Everything* book and saw that he had to first tell the faraway computer that he was getting ready to transfer an ASCII file. The way to do that is to just type

ftp>ascii

The computer responded with another strange message:

200 Type set to A.

That must mean it worked. It should just say "it worked" thought Archie. Oh, well.

The *Everything* book then told him to type **get** followed by the name of the file in double quotation marks. It also said to make sure he typed the letters upper-case when they're listed as uppercase in the directory, and lowercase when they're listed as lowercase in the directory. That's easy.

ftp>get "findme.txt"

The computer responded with an interesting set of messages. First it said

150 Opening ASCII mode data connection for findme (60 bytes)

That must mean it's getting ready to copy it.

After a short pause, the computer said

60 bytes received in .1 seconds (.6 Kbytes/s)

That must mean the file has been transferred over to the Simple Internet computer. Great! It worked!

Bringing the File Down Locally

Archie was ready to finish this FTP session and break off communication between the Simple Internet computer and the faraway computer. Often the word "quit" is used in computers, he had seen, so he tried that here, and it worked:

ftp> quit

The computer responded with

221 Goodbye

That was pretty understandable. Of course, the last thing it says as you disconnect is the only thing that makes sense. Typical computer!

So now to bring the file off the Simple Internet computer and down to his own computer.

The first thing the *Everything* book said to do was to start a *download* session. This meant Archie had to tell the Simple Internet computer that he's ready to copy a file from the Simple Internet computer down to his own computer, over the phone lines. Archie drew Figure 5-6 to help him understand things better.

The *Everything* book explained that there were several ways to do this. The way to download depended on the capabilities of both the computer you're logged into, and the computer you're using.

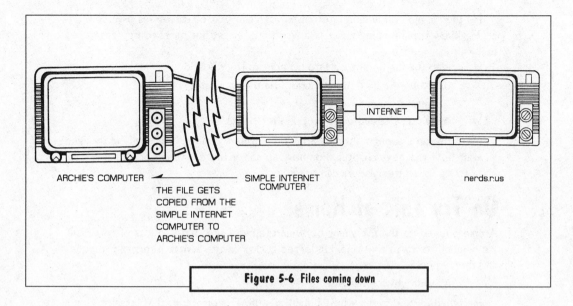

ARCHIE'S COMPUTER

SIMPLE INTERNET
COMPUTER

nerds.r.us

THE FILE GETS
COPIED FROM THE
SIMPLE INTERNET
COMPUTER TO
ARCHIE'S COMPUTER

INTERNET

Figure 5-6 Files coming down

The first one to try, it said, is a method called Zmodem. Archie first had to check on whether his own terminal program supported this thing called Zmodem. He knew that in his case, he should press the (PAGE DOWN) key, and a list of download methods would appear. He knew that the guy at work, who used a Macintosh, pulled down a menu called, perhaps, Transfer, and chose Download or perhaps Receive File, depending on the particular terminal program.

When Archie pressed (PAGE DOWN), he was surprised to see a list that included both Xmodem and ZModem.

The *Everything* book recommended Zmodem, so that's what he'd use. But after the next section he'd read up on how to do it with the others too, just for the experience.

He pressed (ESC) to get rid of the list. He then typed

    sz findme.txt

to tell the Simple Internet computer to start Zmodem and transfer the file called findme.txt over the phone lines so Archie's computer could receive it.

Archie then pressed his (PAGE DOWN) key again, to tell his terminal program to download a file. He selected Zmodem, and then a little message box appeared on his screen telling him the file was coming down.

After only a few moments, the message box went away, meaning the file was on his own computer.

Now he had to tell the Simple Internet computer to go ahead and get rid of the file, since it's been copied down over the phone lines to Archie's own computer. To remove the file from the Simple Internet's computer, Archie typed

    rm findme.txt

He then logged off Simple Internet and ran the text editor on his own computer. He knew that he could also use a word processor, but most computers have a text editor.

He loaded the file findme.txt into his editor. The file said

> **Use Telnet to do a remote login into the computer**
>
> > **missing.covert.com**
>
> **Once there, execute the program FINDME.**

More mystery, thought Archie. Something called "Telnet." Ah, well, he thought. I'll wait until the next chapter. For now I'll see if the *Everything* book has a cool place to ftp to, so the readers can try it, too.

Do Try This at Home

Archie opened up the *Everything* book and found a site that had lots of cool stuff. He decided to ftp to that one. He logged back into the Simple Internet computer, and then typed

> **ftp wuarchive.wustl.edu**

He typed **dir** and saw a whole bunch of stuff. The directory that interested him was pub, just like the last time.

He typed

> **cd pub**

Once inside this directory, he typed **dir** and saw several subdirectories.

He knew that most of these files in these directories weren't ASCII files for reading; rather, they were programs. That meant he had to do something a little different before getting one of the files.

He turned a few more pages in the *Everything* book and discovered that the command to tell the faraway computer to no longer talk ASCII is **binary**. So he typed

> **ftp> binary**

and saw

> **200 Type set to I**

Okay, whatever that means. Maybe someday he'd read one of those big, fat books. But for now he'll just assume that means it's okay.

He typed

> **ftp>get "COOLGAME.EXE"**

Sure enough, a message similar to the earlier ASCII message appeared:

> **150 Opening BINARY mode data connection for COOLGAME.EXE**
> **(2400000 bytes)**

The *Everything* book had warned Archie that some computers had limits on how much you were allowed to pull back from FTP; but apparently the Simple Internet computer wasn't bothered by a file the size of COOLGAME.EXE.

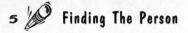

Archie decided this was a good time to look at another method for download-ing files—Xmodem.

For Xmodem, you need to tell the computer what type of file you're down-loading—ASCII or binary.

For downloading ASCII files to all computers except those made by Apple, type

    xmodem st filename

except instead of **filename**, type the name of the file you actually want to down-load. Then start the download from your computer by pressing (PAGE DOWN), or perhaps by pulling down a menu and selecting the proper menu item.

For downloading text files to computers made by Apple, type

    xmodem sa filename

and pull down the appropriate menu.

For all other files, regardless of type of computer, type

    xmodem sb filename

When the file, COOLGAME.EXE, was finally finished downloading to Archie's computer, he could delete it off the Simple Internet computer. He did this by typing

    rm COOLGAME.EXE

and pressing (ENTER) afterwards. Archie figured the letters *rm* were some sort of abbreviation for the word "remove."

So Archie finally had the file COOLGAME.EXE on his computer. He logged out of the Simple Internet computer and started the game by typing **COOLGAME**.

He played it for a while. It wasn't too bad; it had lots of interesting graphics, and it looked like he was inside a building, moving around through the halls. It was all in 3-D, and he encountered all sorts of interesting creatures inside the halls.

A Remote Possibility

A Remote Possibility

The Telnet Connection

Archie was sitting at his computer, finishing up a round of COOLGAME, when he decided it was time to get back to work searching for the missing person.

So he's supposed to do some other thing on the Internet, something called Telnet. Well, he was able to figure out FTP all by himself, so he should be able to figure out this Telnet thing himself.

First, he thought about the context. FTP allowed him to connect to another computer and get files from that computer. Does Telnet do something similar? He looked at the message again:

> **Use Telnet to do a remote login into the computer**
>
> > **missing.covert.com**
>
> **Once there, execute the program FINDME.**

"Use Telnet to do a remote login." He wasn't sure what exactly a remote login was. To log in means to type in your name and password. But the message mentions another computer. Log in to that computer? That's probably what it means. Something about logging into the computer missing.covert.com. Hmm . . . FTP connects to a computer over the Internet. That's it. Telnet must mean he logs into a computer over the Internet.

But that's what he did with FTP. He logged in using FTP. It was anonymously, but he still logged in.

The message, thought Archie, says to execute the program called FINDME. Execute means to run a program. But with FTP he couldn't run a program on that faraway computer, he could only get files off it. Hey, maybe that's the difference. With Telnet he could log into a faraway computer and actually run programs on it.

That made sense to him. He thought about it again. With Telnet, he could log into a faraway computer, over the Internet, and run programs on the other computer. And he had a pretty good idea of what would happen. Everything the faraway computer sent out would appear on his screen, just like when he logs in

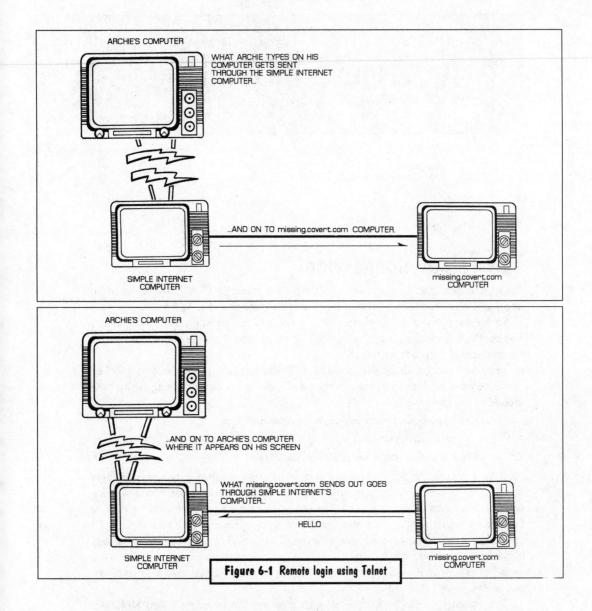

ARCHIE'S COMPUTER

WHAT ARCHIE TYPES ON HIS
COMPUTER GETS SENT
THROUGH THE SIMPLE INTERNET
COMPUTER...

...AND ON TO missing.covert.com COMPUTER.

SIMPLE INTERNET
COMPUTER

missing.covert.com
COMPUTER

ARCHIE'S COMPUTER

...AND ON TO ARCHIE'S COMPUTER
WHERE IT APPEARS ON HIS SCREEN

WHAT missing.covert.com SENDS OUT GOES
THROUGH SIMPLE INTERNET'S
COMPUTER...

HELLO

SIMPLE INTERNET
COMPUTER

missing.covert.com
COMPUTER

Figure 6-1 Remote login using Telnet

over the phone lines to the Simple Internet Connection. And everything he types gets sent over the Internet to that faraway computer.

It's time for a figure, thought Archie. He envisioned Figure 6-1. He included the Simple Internet Connection's computer in the middle, since he was, after all, using it to access the Internet. So everything he typed got sent over the phone line to the Simple Internet computer, and then sent on over the Internet to the faraway computer. And everything that faraway computer sent out over the Internet came into the Simple Internet Connection's computer, and sent out over the phone line to his computer, where it finally appeared on his screen. Cool! Now, thought Archie, I hope I'm not wrong here. Otherwise I wasted an entire figure and several lines of text in this book I'm in!

If Archie was right, he figured Telnet must be a program that runs on the Simple Internet computer, which handles this whole thing. It acts like a middleman in the operation, sending things from either computer to the other. Not too terribly difficult, then.

Archie knew that he had to log into the Simple Internet computer and tell it to run Telnet. After that it was just a matter of executing the program on the remote machine.

But how was he supposed to do that? Well, he knew that to run mail on the Simple Internet computer, he just typed **mail** once he was logged in, and he then pressed (ENTER). And to run FTP on the Simple Internet computer, he just typed **ftp** and pressed (ENTER). So apparently the way to do this was to log into the Simple Internet computer, type **telnet**, and press (ENTER). That would connect him to the faraway computer. Then, since everything he typed would next get sent on to the faraway computer, he could just type the name **FINDME**, and press (ENTER). That would run the program on the remote computer.

Well, it was worth a shot, anyway.

Archie knew that the missing.covert.com computer was a fake computer system made up for this book he's in. So he made a mental note to include some real ones at the end of this chapter.

He dialed into the Simple Internet computer. Once logged in, he typed the word **telnet**. As before with FTP, he remembered to type the name of the computer he was telneting to:

> **telnet missing.covert.com**

The computer responded with,

> **Trying . . .**

and after a few seconds:

> **Connected to missing.covert.com**
> **Escape character is '^]'**
> **SunOS UNIX**
> **login:**

As usual, he didn't worry much about the messages at this point, since they probably weren't very important. He knew that there were big thick books around that could fill in all the gaps. But he wasn't really interested in all that. He just wanted to get the basics, and keep the Internet simple.

So it needed a login name. Archie decided to bring in a new section header in the book he's in.

What Do I Log in As?

Archie was, frankly, clueless as to what to login as. So he checked in the *Everything* book. He dug through several pages until he finally found the section he was looking for. The book said:

> Many computers require you to have an account on them before you log into them, just like you have an account on the Simple Internet computer.

How did the writer know that? thought Archie. Oh, well . . .

> But other computers let just anybody log in. They have a special guest account. Generally the person who tells you about the computer will also give you an account name and password to log in as. If they don't, then you might try the name "guest" with no password.
>
> If you don't have an account on a computer, don't try to get in. If you get into a computer without permission, that's considered a crime, and you can end up in jail. Even if a friend tells you a login and password, and when you connect to the system there's a message prohibiting unauthorized access, it's best not to log in, unless the person who gave it is affiliated with the organization running the computer you're connecting to.

Try "guest" with no password, thought Archie. Sounded like a winner. So he tried it:

> **login: guest**

The computer responded with

> **Welcome to the Superduper People Finder & Scooper.**
>
> **Catch the latest scoop on finding people!**

It worked! He was logged in! It made sense that guest worked, since the person who sent the message didn't give a login name.

Archie wondered what he would have done if guest didn't work. Again, he referred to the *Everything* book:

> You may be wondering what to do if guest doesn't work. Often, in those situations, there will be a message as soon as you connect giving you instructions on how to log in. If not, and guest doesn't work, it's very possible you're not supposed to log in.
>
> Remember also that when logging in, type the login name exactly as given, matching uppercase and lowercase letters. That is, logins are usually case-sensitive.

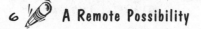

Okay, I'm Logged In

So, he was logged into the faraway computer. He thought again about what that meant. His computer was connected to the Simple Internet computer via the phone lines. The Simple Internet computer was in turn connected to the faraway computer via the Internet. And the Simple Internet computer was using Telnet to send everything Archie typed to the faraway computer, and everything the faraway computer sent back went through the Simple Internet computer and onto his computer's screen.

So now what? He was told to run the program FINDME. That wasn't too difficult. He typed

FINDME

and pressed (ENTER).

Lo and behold, something appeared on his screen. It said

> **Congratulations! You're a better detective than I thought! And for that matter, you're the first person to discover this program! Good job! You're getting warmer!**
>
> **What is your name?**

Okay, thought Archie. It wants to know my name. I wonder if I should use my real name? Yes, he thought, I will use my real name. I don't want to get in trouble for logging into a computer without their knowing who I am. He typed

Archie Finger

and pressed (ENTER).

There was a pause and then the following appeared on his screen:

> **Congratulations, Archie Finger, Private Eye Extraordinaire. You are well on your way to becoming an Internet expert. The next step in your search is to watch the Usenet group soc.internet-people for a message about Birdwatching. This message will be laced with a secret message. (If you don't know how to decode the secret message, get the FAQ on secret messages in the newsgroup alt.secret.decoders.)**
>
> **This computer system has recorded your name and the date and time that you called. So far, you're in the lead to find the missing person. How about a round of GUESSGAME? Y/N**

"Get the FAQ?" What did . . . never mind. Save it for the next chapter, thought Archie.

He knew that the Y/N thing meant he should press either (Y) for yes or (N) for no. So he pressed (Y). The screen cleared and Archie found himself playing an annoying little game where the words "Guess my number" appeared on the screen, and he had to type in a number. He typed in several numbers until it finally said, "You're correct." Then when it asked if he wanted to play another round, he pressed (N).

He logged out of the remote computer by typing

logout

This simply broke off the connection between the Simple Internet computer and the remote computer. Archie still needed to log off the Simple Internet computer. Once again, he typed

logout

and he was logged off completely. He then read in the *Everything* book:

> Sometimes when you have telneted to a remote computer, the way to log off the remote computer may not be immediately apparent. Try the following words:
>
> bye
> quit
> exit
> logout
> logoff
>
> At least one of these should do the trick.

Some Things to Watch Out For

The *Everything* book mentioned a few things people should be aware of when using Telnet. Archie spent a couple of hours reading up on it.

Arriving at the Port

Archie discovered that there are usually several ways to connect remotely to the same computer. These different ways are known as different *ports*, just like a ship might come in through different ports to get to the same country. The *Everything* book said:

> These ports are all numbered. Sometimes when somebody gives you the name of a computer to log into, he or she will also supply a number, such as 10 or 1500. To use this, you type in the name and the number after the Telnet command. For example,
>
> **telnet rafael.metiu.ucsb.edu 5000**
>
> will telnet to "rafael.metiu.ucsb.edu" and connect through its 5000th port, as shown in Figure 6-2.
>
> The reason for this is that sometimes different ports have different uses, and one port might be set aside for exclusive use by the general public.

Archie decided he could handle that. If there's a number called a port, just type it after the site name. Nothing too difficult there.

He turned the computer off and went upstairs to watch a videotape. It was a comedy that had absolutely nothing to do with computers. He figured he needed that after a long, hard day's work.

Figure 6-2 Connecting to Port 5000 of site rafael.metiu.ucsb.edu

The next morning, after a good night's sleep, before he went into work, Archie logged into the Simple Internet computer to check the soc.internet-people group, and, lo and behold, there was a message on birdwatchers. It said, "I'm trying to contact a friend of mine who's into birdwatching. Does anybody have his address?" There were also about 30 angry messages that followed saying things like, "Well, we can't help you if you don't give his name, you fool," and "Sure, I'll give you his Internet address, as soon as you give us his stinking name!"

Archie reread the first message and noticed a string of letters at the bottom that went

vzsbgahqcrenqgnqrd

Hmm . . . thought Archie. That looks like a secret message.

Garbage Onscreen

Archie saw in the *Everything* book:

> Sometimes when you log into a system, you will be asked for Terminal Type. Generally, the question will include in parentheses (vt100 ok?). In many cases, you can just press (ENTER) and go on. But if you do, and what ends up on your screen is a mess of letters and numbers that don't make sense (and sometimes you can see words mixed in), then the remote computer probably isn't sending the characters over the Internet in a form your computer is expecting. If that's the case, you can try typing **ANSI** and see if that works.
>
> Sometimes, though, you won't be given a choice. If that's the case, you may need to change the Terminal Type from within your terminal

program. (For Macs and Windows computers, there's probably a menu item; for DOS and other command-line-type computers, there's probably a key sequence, such as (ALT)-(T).) Then you can choose a different kind of terminal. You may have to guess and just try different ones until you find the one that works. Sometimes, though, you may not even find one that works. In these cases, you might not be able to log into that particular system.

Little Annoyances

The *Everything* book had a section called "Small Inconveniences." It said

Sometimes when you telnet to a system, you'll have things happen like seeing a message that says "Press space to continue," and when you press (SPACEBAR), nothing happens. If this happens, try pressing (ENTER) after pressing (SPACEBAR). Sometimes the remote system needs a little "kick" before responding to the spacebar.

Other times you may see something like "Press the down-arrow," and when you do, nothing happens. For instance, you may see a list of numbered items with sort of a pointer —> pointing to an item. Pressing ⬇ is supposed to move the pointer down one item. But when you press ⬇, nothing happens. In these cases, the menu items will usually have numbers beside them, and you should be able to type the number for the item you want. You may have to press (ENTER) afterwards; it's best to first type the number and wait a moment. If nothing happens, then press (ENTER).

Escape from Telnet

Archie decided that he had learned enough to figure out what the line he saw when he logged in,

Escape character is '^]'

was all about. He knew that the word "escape" meant to break out of a computer program, and on many computers there was actually a key labeled Esc, for escape. So he figured what this meant was if things weren't going well for some reason, he could get out of Telnet by typing something.

He remembered seeing that ^ (caret) symbol in some computer books when he was younger. He knew that referred to the control key, labeled Ctrl. So he knew this all meant that if he needed to suddenly get out of Telnet, he could hold down (CTRL) and press ⏑, the right-bracket key.

Archie looked in the *Everything* book and saw:

Indeed, you are correct. When you do a remote login through Telnet, there will usually be a message telling you what the escape character is. The ^ (caret) means the (CTRL) key. Generally the escape character is either ^], meaning to hold down (CTRL) and press ⏑, or ^\, meaning to hold down (CTRL) and press ⟍ (backslash). (Note that although you're pressing two keys—(CTRL) and (1), for instance—the combination is known as a single *character*.)

The times you may need to escape are when, for example, the remote computer seems to freeze up, or if the remote computer just plain takes too long to do anything. Or you might run a program on the remote computer that prevents you from being able to log out.

Do Try This at Home

If your Internet connection supports Telnet, you can try doing a remote login into various computers.

Here are some real sites you might try telneting to.

telnet astro.temple.edu 12345

Note that in this case, you're telneting into port 12345 of astro.temple.edu. When you connect, a famous quote will print on your screen, and then the remote computer will automatically disconnect.

Here are a couple of Telnet sites maintained by NASA:

telnet spacelink.msfc.nasa.gov

and

telnet nssdc.gsfc.nasa.gov

The first doesn't ask for a login or password. For the second, log in as **nodis**. There's no password for the second, either.

CHAPTER 7

Just the FAQs:
More on File Transfer

Just the FAQs: More on File Transfer

Archie was tired. He put down half of the bagel he was munching on and stared at the computer screen. It seemed like nearly his whole life these days was spent in front of the computer. And worse, it felt like he was going on a wild goose chase, only an electronic form of one. Here he was supposed to be looking for a missing person, and he had hardly budged from the computer.

"Get the FAQ." What was a FAQ? He guessed that it was pronounced like "fak." After all, computer people liked to pronounce acronyms rather than spell them out.

He had seen the word "FAQ" when he was rummaging through the Usenet groups: People would ask where the FAQ was located, or would tell others to read the FAQ before posting a basic question about whatever topic the news-group was about.

So apparently a FAQ talked about beginner's questions? That would make sense in all the contexts that he had seen it. But what did it stand for? Q probably stood for question. Not too many words begin with Q. But what did the F and A stand for? He looked in the *Everything* book, and it appeared that the book didn't have everything. There was no entry in the index for the word "FAQ."

So he logged onto the Simple Internet Connection and went to the Secret Decoder newsgroup, alt.secret.decoder. There were lots of different messages, many with strange subjects, such as "How to use the AX9-B7 decoder after the 321A decoder," and "I hate decoding," and "Where's the FAQ?"

Where's the FAQ, thought Archie. That's the one I need. He read the message. It said:

Where is the FAQ for this newsgroup?

Yeah, good question, thought Archie. But what on earth is a FAQ? Why didn't the poster say something like "Where is the FAQ, which, for those of you who don't know, is a blah blah blah?" Unfortunately, nobody had replied yet to this message.

He read through a few more postings and finally, at the bottom of a reply to an article called "How do I use T-16-42 Decoder," found something that said

> The Frequently Asked Question paper can be found posted here in this newsgroup about once a month. For all you beginners to this topic, please read the FAQ before posting beginners' questions. That helps prevent the same question from getting posted a hundred times a day. Note that the FAQ for this newsgroup gets updated every week.

So that's it: FAQ stands for Frequently Asked Questions. And these FAQs are used to supply answers to beginners' questions. Apparently there's only one per newsgroup, and they get updated periodically. So all Archie needed to do is get hold of the FAQ on decoders and figure out how to decode the strange message he received the other day. Cool!

He dug through the messages in the alt.secret.decoder newsgroup and finally managed to find the FAQ. There was a lot of boring information in the FAQ about the mathematics behind decoding things. But near the bottom he found a strange set of instructions:

> One lesser-known method of decoding is particularly useful to detectives looking for missing people. The way to do it is to take the first letter of each word in the message and increase the letter by one. (That is, *a* becomes *b*, *b* becomes *c*, and so on. Note that *z* becomes *a*.)

Okay, thought Archie. That must be for him. He looked at the message he was trying to decode:

vzsbgahqcrenqgnqrd

He grabbed a sheet of paper and decoded it. The resulting message said

watchbirdsforhorse

He could break it up to get

watch birds for horse

What does that mean? Watch birds? For a horse? He thought about it, and it was clear to him that this is all happening over the Internet, so he must have to watch some sort of birds group or something. He'd better get a list of all the newsgroups and try and find one relating to birds.

Do Try This at Home

If you want to get a FAQ for a newsgroup, you can post a message on the newsgroup asking where the FAQ is. FAQs are generally posted to the newsgroups from time to time, but they are often archived on an FTP site. Another place where real Usenet groups place their FAQs is in the news.answers Usenet group. If you watch this group for a while, you'll see lots of FAQs getting posted every day.

If you have an Internet connection, you can ftp to

ftp rtfm.mit.edu

and look in the pub directory to find several FAQs. Unfortunately, this particular system only allows 50 connections at any given time, so it's very difficult to log into. Another place you can ftp to is

ftp.uu.net

and look in the usenet directory. There are subdirectories underneath this one for different FAQs.

Note that these are saved in a special form on the disk drive to save space; this is called compressed. To get them uncompressed, so that you can read them, ask for the file without the .Z at the end.

For instance, if there's a file called

one.Z

you would type

get "one"

without the .Z. That will tell the remote system to decompress it before sending it.

Squished, Squeezed, and Compressed

In the *Everything* book Archie saw a section called "Compressed Files." According to the book, it's possible to save files on a disk in a manner that takes up less space than they normally would. This is called *compression*: The file gets compressed before it's saved on the disk, similar to what's happening in Figure 7-1.

According to the *Everything* book, there are several forms of compression, and generally a compressed file ends with a period followed by one, two, or three letters. These letters denote the type of compression used.

Figure 7-1 *Archie compresses a file to make it smaller*

For instance, a file may be called

tetris.zip

which means it's compressed using a zip method. Other file name endings are

arc

sit

Z

zoo

The arc and zip endings are generally for MS-DOS computers; sit is for Macs. The Z is for Unix, and zoo is for lots of different computers, including MS-DOS. There are programs available for all these machines that decompress the files.

There's another way of storing files that converts binary files into an ASCII form that can be sent over email. This form is called uuencoded (often pronounced "you-you-encoded"). These files usually won't show up in FTP directories; rather, they'll be inside email messages or Usenet news items.

The *Everything* book pointed out that if you see a mail message filled with a huge block of letters, with most lines starting with an *M*, then this is probably a uuencoded message.

To decode it, save the email message to a file and run a program called uudecode. For MS-DOS computers, this looks like this:

uudecode filename

What happens is the reverse of the uuencode process.

The *Everything* book said that FTP sites will often do the hard part of decompressing a file before sending it over FTP. That means when you receive it, it'll already be uncompressed and you won't have to worry about it. Unfortunately, it's generally only for the Z compression. To retrieve the uncompressed files so that you can read it, ask for the file without the .Z at the end.

For instance, if there's a file called

one.Z

you would type

get "one"

without the .Z. That will tell the faraway system to decompress it before sending it.

I Don't Have FTP

Archie had become concerned earlier that the Simple Internet computer didn't have FTP, but was pleased to see it did. He wondered, though, what he would do if he didn't have it.

The *Everything* book mentioned that it's possible to get files through FTP even if you don't have FTP. The way to do it is to send email to a certain computer that offers FTP by mail. After this computer receives the email message, *it* will run FTP for you, get the file, and email a copy to you. (If it's a binary file, it'll come uuen-coded.)

There are at least two such FTP-by-mail servers out there. People in North America can use

       ftp@decwrl.dec.com

and people in Europe and elsewhere can use

       ftpmail@grasp.insa-lyon.fr

Archie decided he'd try to get the same file he retrieved earlier using real FTP:

       mail ftp@decwrl.dec.com
       subject:
       connect nerds.r.us
       chdir "/pub/secret"
       get findme.txt
       quit

He sent the message off and waited. It took a day or so, but eventually the file came; when Archie logged in a day later he found he had email, and the body of the email was the file he requested.

The *Everything* book said you can also get binary files. In these cases, the body of the email message should look like this:

       connect sitename
       chdir "directory"
       binary
       uuencode
       get filename
       quit

Here you would replace **sitename** with the site you're trying to access; **"directory"** with the full directory, as in **"/pub/secret"**; and **filename** with the actual file name, such as **coolgame.exe**.

You can also request a listing of all files in a directory:

       connect sitename
       chdir "directory"
       binary
       dir
       quit

Finally, you can request help by simply typing

       help

for the body of the email message.

Some Catches to FTP by Mail

There are some catches with doing FTP by mail. For one, the system you log into may not allow you to receive huge email messages, and the file you're trying to have mailed to you may be too big.

Another problem is the delay. This actually causes two problems. You may not know what's in a directory, and since everything is going over email, when you request a directory, you have to wait for it to come.

Still, FTP by mail is handy if you don't have access to FTP.

Still More Groups

Still More Groups

Archie needed a list of all the newsgroups. As it happened, the computer he logged into, the Simple Internet Connection, had a list online that he could look at or download to his own machine.

There were actually two lists: One was called Usenet and one was called Local. He downloaded both lists and printed them.

Two Kinds of Groups

The Usenet list was divided into two main types. The first type was Usenet; the second was Alternate. There was a short note at the beginning of the list, explaining the difference.

The note explained that Usenet was technically a set of rules upheld voluntarily by a group of people. These rules outlined what must be done to create a newsgroup. But it said that news is really just massive amounts of information getting copied from computer to computer, and if two people owning computers want to copy information between their computers, who can stop them?

So people started making their own newsgroups that weren't part of this thing called Usenet. These newsgroups are called the alternate newsgroups. And these newsgroups aren't bound by the rules of Usenet; so pretty much any topic, no matter how controversial or offensive, can appear in these alternate newsgroups. Many people still refer to these alternate groups as Usenet news, but technically they aren't part of Usenet, as Figure 8-1 illustrates.

Usenet Newsgroups

Archie noticed that all the Usenet newsgroups in the list started with one of the following:

comp

news

rec

sci

soc

talk

misc

The note in the file explained that the comp groups were all about computers. The news groups were for discussions about Internet news and newsgroups. The rec groups were all about hobbies and recreation, and music and arts. The sci groups were all about different sorts of sciences, while the talk groups held discussions and debates about all sorts of topics. The misc groups were for things that didn't fit into any of the others.

Alternate Newsgroups

The note explained that there are different types of alternate newsgroups. Some are local to a certain geographic area, and people who own computers in that area generally get the newsgroup. Others started out as private discussion groups on a computer system where lots of users log into, and eventually the private group started getting copied out to another computer—and more and more computers—until a good share of the computers on the Internet started getting the newsgroups.

Archie saw lots of newsgroups in this alternate section. Most of them started with the word "alt." But some of them started with other words. There was a brief explanation for the other prefixes:

Figure 8-1 Usenet and Alternate news

bionet	Groups that start with this carry news about biology.
bit	These groups are the same as some of the bitnet lists mentioned in Chapter 4.
biz	These are groups for business. Ads sometimes show up here.
courts	These are about the law.
clarinet	This is the United Press International and several syndicated columns, such as Dave Barry. It's available to a computer system by subscription only.
de	Discussions in German.
fj	Discussions in Japanese.
hepnet	Newsgroups relating to high-energy physics.
ieee	Groups for Institute of Electrical and Electronics Engineers.
k12	Education, particularly kindergarten through 12th grade.
relcom	Discussions in Russian.
vmsnet	Groups for discussing things about VAX/VMS computers.

The note added that these are just a few; there are many more, and of these, some may not be carried on every computer.

Some for All, Some for Some

Archie was starting to get a feel for how the newsgroup thing worked. There are two types of groups, Usenet and Alternate, and Usenet is bound by a set of rules, while the Alternate isn't. The Alternate is more of a free-form style of news, and these alternate groups don't appear on all computers that get news. Some aren't even available in that part of the country, while some are, but the owner of the computer system carrying the news doesn't care to have that group sent onto his or her computer.

Archie added to this line of thinking his thoughts in an earlier chapter about how news actually works. It's sort of like email, except "messages" get sent out to lots and lots of computers, and are available for reading by most of the users logging into these computers.

The news doesn't go to all computers on the Internet; only certain ones allowed to receive that group, and of those computers, only the ones whose owners want to receive the particular newsgroup. Also, the clarinet groups in particular can only get sent to a computer system for a fee.

It's Been a Long Time

Archie knew from Chapter 2 that news expires after a while. He found a brief note about this in the *Everything* book. Each news item takes up a certain amount of space on a hard drive, and the more news that appears on the computer, the more space gets taken up. That means, to keep disk space open, the computer that's receiving the news will often delete old news as new news arrives. This act of deleting news is called "expiring" the news.

The computer Archie gets news from, the Simple Internet Connection, expires news after about three days. The *Everything* book said that some computers carry news for two weeks or more, while some carry it only for a day or so before it gets expired. Every computer is different, and the amount of time it sits around on the disk depends on the size of the disk, and how long the person who owns the computer feels it's safe to keep it around without eating up too much disk space.

For Some People's Eyes Only

Archie found something else that caught his interest in the *Everything* book. Sometimes a person will post a news item, and he or she feels it's somewhat distasteful, but still wants to send it out. To make people pause before reading it and think about whether they really want to read it, the person posting it uses a simple form of encryption similar to the type Archie's missing person used. This encryption is called "rot13," for rotate 13. It simply means each letter is bumped forward by 13 letters, so *A* becomes *N*, *B* becomes *O*, and so on. Numbers and things like periods and spaces and other nonletters don't get changed. Here are all the conversions:

```
A  B  C  D  E  F  G  H  I  J  K  L  M
|  |  |  |  |  |  |  |  |  |  |  |  |
N  O  P  Q  R  S  T  U  V  W  X  Y  Z
```

This table works two ways. The first line says *A* translates to *N*, and that *N* translates to *A*.

The *Everything* book said you can easily spot a rot13-encrypted message, because it'll look just like garbled text. There was an example in the *Everything* book,

> Guvf vf na rapelcgrq zrffntr!

which translates to

> This is an encrypted message!

As Archie was looking at this encryption scheme, he noticed something interesting about it. If he took a word, such as "hello," and translated it, he got the letters *uryyb*. But to decode it, all he had to do was translate it again—*u* translates to *h*, which is right back where it started.

So that means when you translate something manually, you don't need to worry about which way to go.

The *Everything* book explained that many computers will have this encryption scheme built in, so you don't have to try and do it yourself. For the standard Unix mail program the way to decode a message is to press (SHIFT)-(D). The book also said that this encryption scheme is generally used in the rec.humor Usenet group. Most alternate groups don't bother with encrypting the messages. People expect them to be off-color or offensive to begin with.

The *Everything* book mentioned that different mail- and news-reader programs have different ways of decrypting and encrypting these messages. For the nn news-reader, you press (SHIFT)-(D) when reading a news item to decrypt it.

The Missing Newsgroup

Archie was digging through the list of alternate groups, when he stumbled upon the group rec.birds. That had to do with birds. Maybe that was the newsgroup in question.

He logged onto the Simple Internet computer and joined the group rec.birds. There was a message there with the heading

birdwatching while riding a horse

The rather long-winded message was about taking a ride on horseback through the Great Plains in the Midwest, and watching for unusual birds. It didn't particularly strike Archie's interest, but he read it anyway. Towards the end, there was a name. It was Gloria Strysdale. This time, however, it occurred to him to look at the From section of the news item. It said

strysdale@super.geeks.com

So Gloria *is* somehow connected to the supergeeks place where the original email message went. Hmm . . . this is starting to get interesting, thought Archie.

Try This

Here are some newsgroups you can check out. Note that this is only a partial listing of all the groups.

Usenet Newsgroups
Comp Groups

> comp.answers, comp.archives.msdos.announce,
> comp.sys.mac.announce

Misc Groups

> misc.answers, misc.consumers, misc.forsale, misc.jobs.misc,
> misc.jobs.offered, misc.writing

News Groups (Groups about Usenet)

news.answers, news.groups

Rec Groups

Each of these starts with rec, as in *rec.answers*.

answers, audio.high-end, autos, running, windsurfing

Rec.Arts Groups

All of these start with rec.arts; for instance, *rec.arts.animation*.

animation, books, sf.written, startrek.misc, theatre

Rec.Crafts Groups

All of these start with rec.crafts, such as *rec.crafts.jewelry*.

jewelry, metalworking

Rec.Food

All of these start with rec.food; for instance, *rec.food.cooking*.

cooking, recipes, veg.cooking

Rec.Games Groups

All of these begin with rec.games; for example, *rec.games.backgammon*.

backgammon, mud.announce, video.arcade, video.sega

Rec.Music Groups

There are lots of groups about different types of music and different musicians. Each of these starts with rec.music, such as *rec.music.beatles*.

beatles, bluenote, makers, makers.guitar

Rec.Sports Groups

All of these start with rec.sport, as in *rec.sport.baseball*.

baseball, basketball.misc, football.misc

Sci Groups

All of these start with sci, as in *sci.fractals*.

fractals, nanotech, physics

Soc Groups

soc.college, soc.politics, soc.singles

Soc.Culture Groups

There are several groups that begin with soc.culture, followed by a place, such as *soc.culture.african* and *soc.culture.mexican*.

Groups about People on the Net

soc.net-people, soc.penpals

Talk Groups

talk.abortion, talk.environment, talk.philosophy.misc

Alternate Newsgroups

Here are some alternate newsgroups. Since not all of these are carried by every computer system on the Internet, the system you log into may not get some of these. (Some systems don't carry *any* alternate groups.)

> **alt.answers, alt.books.reviews, alt.business.misc, alt.comics.superman, alt.consumers.free-stuff, alt.cyberpunk, alt.genealogy, alt.guitar, alt.missing-kids, alt.personals.ads, alt.zines**

These groups all start with alt.fan, as in *alt.fan.dave-barry*.

> **dave-barry, douglas-adams, frank-zappa, monty-python**

These groups all start with alt.games, as in *alt.games.doom*.

> **doom, torg, vga-planets, video.classic**

These all start with alt.music, as in *alt.music.jethro-tull*.

> **jethro-tull, marillion, misc, pearl-jam, peter-gabriel, pink-floyd, todd-rundgren**

These groups all start with alt.politics, as in *alt.politics.british*.

> **british, clinton, datahighway**

These groups all start with alt.sport, as in *alt.sport.bowling*.

> **bowling, jet-ski, racquetball**

These groups all start with alt.sports (note the plural sports, whereas the previous was singular!) as in *alt.sports.baseball.atlanta-braves*.

> **baseball.atlanta-braves, baseball.chicago-cubs, baseball.detroit-tigers**

These all start with alt.tv, as in *alt.tv.babylon-5*.

> **babylon-5, game-shows, mash, seinfeld**

Clarinet Groups

Here are some of the clarinet groups:

> **clari.biz.commodity, clari.biz.urgent, clari.feature.davebarry, clari.nb.apple, clari.net.announce, clari.news.books, clari.news.consumer, clari.news.goodnews, clari.news.gov, clari.news.headlines, clari.news.weather**

If the system you log into doesn't get the clarinet newsgroups, but you want to, you can find out subscription information by sending email to

> **info@clarinet.com**

with a blank subject and body.

CHAPTER 9

In-laws, Outlaws, and
Net Law

THE·LAW·OF·THE·INTERNET

In-laws, Outlaws, and Net Law

Archie wasn't going to sit around waiting for more news. This time he was just gonna do something about it. He was gonna send email to Gloria, now that he'd found her. Either that or he could wait until next time she came by to clean his place, but somehow he doubted she would.

Of course, maybe the regular maid, Susan, who Archie had never met, would come by next time. Wait, thought Archie. I have an idea. I'm gonna first contact this Susan person.

He phoned the maid service, and the same nasal-voiced woman answered. "Acme. Can I help you?"

"Yes, I'd like to speak to Susan."

"Let me see if she's here."

There was a pause, then a young woman's voice. "Hello?"

"Hi, is this Susan?"

"Yes it is." Her voice was rather timid.

"This is Archie Finger. You're supposedly the person who's been cleaning my place for a few weeks now, but you haven't."

"Well, um . . ." Her voice was shaky. "I, um, had a substitute come to your place. Gloria."

"Aha!" said Archie. He heard a small squeak of panic from the other end of the line.

"I'm sorry sir," she said. "But she paid me. Uh-oh, my boss is glaring. I gotta go. Bye!" She hung up the phone.

So, thought Archie. Susan probably isn't really involved. Somehow, Gloria knew that I was getting a maid service, and that this would be a good way to get into my house and teach me some Internet stuff. But how did she know I was getting a maid service? Nobody knew that. Nobody's been in here, except . . . except Veronica!

He thought about that. Veronica could easily have seen the note he wrote on his pad next to the computer about calling Acme Maid Service. She could have called to find out who was scheduled to clean the place, and then have Gloria pay off the girl and take her place.

So Veronica is involved in all this. That made perfect sense. After all, it was her *friend* who disappeared.

Archie logged onto the Simple Internet computer and began composing an email message to strysdale@super.geeks.com. He wrote

> **I'm starting to put things together. I'm no longer gonna go on this wild goose chase to find this missing person. You know where he is, and you probably knew all along. Tell me where he is.**

He then saved it. It's gone, he thought to himself. Off to Gloria. But gosh, she's such a nice lady. Maybe I shouldn't talk to her in such a mean tone. I'll just . . . just what? It's gone. It's been sent out. Oops. Archie started to sweat a little. Gosh, I hope I don't make her mad. I'd better remember this. Never send an email message out without carefully thinking about it. It's too easy to rush something out and then regret it.

His mind started wandering, and he thought about how easy it would be to do just such a thing on Usenet, for everyone to see. That could be a bad situation, he thought. I wonder if there are any rules about what you can and can't say on Usenet?

Rules, Rules, Rules

Archie grabbed the *Everything* book and began paging through it. There was an entire chapter on ethics. The beginning said

> Most computer systems that carry news will have a file that you're supposed to download and read before posting any news. It's a good idea to do this, because if you do something you're not supposed to, the owner of the computer system you're logging into to get news can get in trouble, possibly causing everyone who logs into that system to lose their news privileges.

Wow, thought Archie. That sounds pretty scary. He was still logged into the Simple Internet computer. He remembered seeing a file called rules next to the file that lists all the newsgroups. That was probably the file that the *Everything* book was referring to. He downloaded it and printed it. Here's what it said:

> Welcome to Simple Internet News! We're happy to have you post and receive news, but there are a few rules you have to abide by. Remember that if you violate these rules, the Simple Internet Connection could be held liable, and you could cause all the other users of Simple Internet to lose their privileges.

Rule 1: Stick to the Topic

Don't talk about another topic in the group; take it to the appropriate group. Don't talk about whether the topic is appropriate; if you feel it's not, then don't read the group. Don't post to multiple groups, because each group is for a separate topic, so your topic probably doesn't fit into both groups.

Rule 2: Tone of Voice

Don't type messages in all capital letters: IT SOUNDS LIKE YOU ARE SHOUTING OR ANGRY. Also, it's very easy to sound like you're angry as all get out and beyond belief and would like to murder the person who is reading your mail or posting mail. You may use strong language and mean it only a little bit strong, but the reader may feel like you're getting violent. If you say something that's a joke or to be taken in jest, tack on the smiley :-) It's a good way to remind people, "That was a joke," or, "No, I'm not really that mad."

Rule 3: No Flaming

If someone says or does something inappropriate, SUCH AS TYPING IN ALL CAPS, don't post a response *flaming* them—that is, don't send an angry message insulting them. Either ignore it or send private email to the person. (Ignoring it might be best, because it's quite likely the person will get private mail from hundreds of other people griping about the same thing.) Also, never threaten anybody on the Internet. A threat can be taken seriously, and you could wind up in jail. And especially don't post a message claiming you're going to do something illegal or something that will violate national security or anything like that. There was an incident in North Carolina where somebody posted a message claiming they were going to kill the president. In almost no time at all, the Secret Service showed up and arrested the person.

Rule 4: Abide by Copyright Laws

Don't post copyrighted material. Remember also that posting is a form of publication, so if you have some original material, such as a short story, think twice before posting it. However, if you would like to use a posting as a method for publishing something you've written, you may want to consult with a lawyer first.

Rule 5: Keep it Neat

Many people's computers are limited to 80 columns of text. If yours is more, try and keep the lines in your messages shorter than 80 columns so these people can read them. Also, it's acceptable to left-justify a message, but don't right-justify. This makes it difficult to read.

Rule 6: Lots of People Are Out There

Remember, there are real people reading your postings—lots of real people—so be careful what you say and think twice before posting. It's easy to quickly write a message and send it out, and then realize you said something you didn't mean to, or said something you probably shouldn't have. And once it's posted, it's posted for all to see.

Rule 7: Use Appropriate Subjects and Follow-ups

When filling in the subject line, write an appropriate subject so that readers can see exactly what your message is about and skip it if they don't want to read it. Many readers will immediately skip over a message with a header such as "READ THIS!" or a blank header. If your message is a response to someone else's, you might include a couple lines of the other message (follow-up lines) to remind readers what you're responding to. But keep it to only a few lines of follow-up. A good rule of thumb is to make sure there are fewer follow-up lines than original lines. Remember also that if you're answering a specific question, it's very possible others will answer, too. You may want to consider sending private email rather than a posting.

Rule 8: Don't Post Advertisements

Posting of advertisements violates Usenet regulations. If you own a business, don't expect to use the Internet for free advertising. Also, don't send email advertising products unless the recipient has already given you permission.

Rules for FTP and Telnet

The *Everything* book had some rules that dealt with FTP and Telnet.

Rule 1: Downloading Software

Do not download software that's intended for retail sale from a computer. Such software is "pirated" and is illegal to have and illegal to download. Whoever owns the computer is already breaking the law if there's such software on it, and if you download it, you're breaking the law, too. The Federal Bureau of Investigation (FBI) handles such cases, and the penalties are severe. You may end up like the person in Figure 9-1.

Rule 2: New Users

Sometimes computers don't have a guest account, but do allow new users to register. If you telnet to a computer and it asks for your real name, phone number, and address, either give the correct information or disconnect. If you give fake information, this may be considered illegal entry into a computer system, and the FBI would take it from there.

Rule 3: Don't Break In

If you are not given access to log into a computer, and it does not have a guest account, does not allow anonymous FTP, and does not allow new users, do not try to break into the computer. It may seem like fun at first to try different names and passwords, but the fun will end when the FBI comes knocking on your door and hauls you off to jail. Breaking into a computer is a crime. This applies to calling into a computer over phone lines, telneting to a computer, and ftping to a computer. Fortunately, a good share of computers on the Internet allow anonymous FTP, or have a guest login account for Telnet. If they don't, don't try to get in unless you've explicitly been given an account on the computer.

Rule 4: Read the FAQs

When you ftp to a computer and see a file called readme, it's a good idea to grab the file and read it.

Rule 5: Follow the Rules

Each computer you log into will have its own set of rules, and these rules will probably be shown when you log in. Follow the rules. You're logged into their system, so you have to abide by their rules.

Rule 6: Upgrades Via FTP

Sometimes you may see a file available on FTP, and a notice (such as in a readme file) stating that to download the file you must have obtained a license for the software. Such cases are common for software upgrades made available over FTP—you must have the original software before you're allowed to retrieve the upgrade file that's available. In these situations it's possible for you to ftp the file, and chances are, nobody will stop you. However, if you do, you're in violation of copyright laws, and once again the FBI may come pay you a visit.

Rule 7: Encryption

Be careful sending encrypted files outside the country. The National Security Agency may get a little nervous.

Figure 9-1 A net law violator

Rule 8: Virus Alert

Be careful when downloading programs. There are certain types of programs out there called viruses that can cause damage to your computer. Some viruses cause damage to your hardware, and some do things like wipe out files from your hard drive. There are a few thousand types of viruses, and most hide themselves inside other programs. It's very possible when you download a program that it contains a virus, even if the program you're getting seems benign, such as a simple game. There are commercially available programs that you can buy in software stores or get through the mail that test for viruses and eliminate them if they find any. Viruses are very real and are a major problem, and virus-checking programs are an essential part of having your own computer. Also, it's best to retrieve a program from the FTP site maintained by the software company that produced the program, or from the site recommended by the software company.

Rule 9: Password Choices

If you're logging into a computer for the first time and the computer asks you to choose a password, choose one that you can remember, and one that other people aren't likely to discover. Don't use the name of your spouse or child for a password; don't use your telephone number, or anything that might be obvious, such as simple words like pencil or paper. And don't tell anybody your password. Don't fall for the old trick of someone calling you and saying they work for the Internet and need to know your password. Nobody should ever call you asking for your password. And don't email your password to anybody else, because not only should they not need it, but sending it over the email may not be private. It's too easy for others to get their hands on the email message.

Rule 10: Summary

Use common sense and common courtesy.

Archie stopped reading and let everything sink in. That's a lot of rules, he told himself.

Now I have to think about catching up with both Gloria and Veronica, he thought to himself. He logged onto Simple Internet and checked his email. There was a message! The From name was strange; it was from someone Archie didn't recognize:

> imgreat@covert.com.

The message said

> Watch the windsurfing newsgroup for a question about favorite
> places to windsurf in Oregon.
> Sincerely,
> Max Von Veign
> Internet Guru Extraordinaire

"This is getting strange," said Archie.

Cool Things

Cool Things

Archie was wading through more and more postings in the group called rec.windsurfing. He found nothing on the topic of favorite places to windsurf in Oregon. Lots of talk about favorite brands of boards, and so on, but nothing on places in Oregon. At one point someone posted a message on favorite places to windsurf, and Archie thought that was it, but then the person said she's in New England.

He nearly gave up, when he happened to read a message on places to buy boards out west. Then he noticed a note at the bottom of the posting:

> I live in California and would like recommendations on the best places in the L.A. area to buy windsurfing boards. Also, I'm planning a trip to Oregon this summer, and would like to do a bit of windsurfing while I'm there. Can anybody recommend any places?

Archie glanced at the top and saw the address

> ab15323@anon.penet.fi

He particularly noticed the word "anon." Could that mean anonymous? Indeed, there was no name anywhere in the message. Can you do that? If Archie posts a message, his name appears at the top of the message, alongside his email address.

Anonymous Postings

Archie knew that when he types a message, he doesn't fill in his name. The Simple Internet computer does that part automatically. I suppose, thought Archie, I could have given them a fake name when I signed up. But I've heard that that's bad—it could be treated as an illegal entry into a computer system, which is a violation of federal law. The last thing he needed was to go to jail for the sake of sending out anonymous postings!

Apparently there was a computer system set up specifically for anonymous postings. Archie saw a note at the very bottom of the posting that said

> To find out more about the anon service, send mail to
> help@anon.penet.fi. Due to the double-blind, any mail replies to
> this message will be anonymous, and an anonymous id will be
> allocated automatically. You have been warned. Please report
> any problems, inappropriate use, etc. to admin@anon.penet.fi.

Double-blind? That's an odd term. Judging by the little write-up that follows, *double-blind* must mean you don't know who you're replying to if you reply to that message, and the recipient doesn't know who you are, either. Both the To and From become anonymous IDs.

So that's how it works. He could send email to admin@anon.penet.fi and get information on how this anonymous posting service works. But he had a pretty good idea. He was starting to understand how all this Internet stuff worked, so this one was easy. The anonymous posting service would probably give him an account. Then to send mail out, he could just send email to the computer that the posting service is on, and it would in turn send out a duplicate email message from his account on that computer. And it wouldn't fill in his real name at the top.

He thought about how he might receive mail. Probably, if someone sent mail to his anonymous account, the computer there would in turn send the email message on to his own real account at Simple Internet.

He considered sending email to admin@anon.penet.fi, but decided first he'd look around through the news messages and see if anyone else was posting anonymously. Maybe there are other anonymous servers, and he could collect a list of them.

He looked through the windsurfing group, but didn't see any other anonymous postings. So he grabbed his list of groups and rummaged through it. He noticed one called alt.personals.ads. That sounds like a place where there would be anonymous postings!

He joined the group and saw a list of message headers that were recently posted. Here are a few of them:

> **SWF, 25, seeks SWM**
>
> **SBM seeks good time in Chicago**
>
> **Looking for a SWM**
>
> **A Single BF is available!**

He looked at the first message. It was from

> **abc-10254@chop.ucsd.edu**

and there was no mention of a person's name in the posting. At the bottom of the posting was the message

> **For information on how to use the Anonymous Contact Service,
> send email to acs-info@chop.ucsd.edu.**

So that's another anonymous service. That's interesting, thought Archie. Seems a bit unethical to send out anonymous postings, but these are, of course, the alternative newsgroups, so it must be okay.

Archie knew it would probably take a couple days for the information to come if he sent email to these places. But, since I'm living in a book, thought Archie, I'll let the readers try it themselves. All they have to do is send a blank email message to either of the services mentioned. Since the recipient is just a computer, it automatically replies with information on the service.

However, he decided to send email to the person who posted the first message at the beginning of this chapter. There was supposed to be an encrypted message at the bottom of the posting, but there wasn't. Maybe Archie was supposed to send email to the person and await an encrypted message.

But what should the email say? He thought about it and decided to make the email say, "I see the real meaning of your message. Send me some email!"

So he went back to the windsurfing groups, pulled up the same message, and pressed the (SHIFT)-(M) key to compose an email message. He typed

I see the real meaning of your message. Send me some email!

He typed a period on a blank line, and then pressed (ENTER) when asked what to do next, and the mail was on its way.

Now all he had to do was await a reply. That meant he had some more time on his hands. To do what? To play of course!

Bitnet Lists

The *Everything* book had a chapter called "Interesting Things." Archie thought some of the stuff looked pretty cool, so he decided to try it.

The Current Weather

The first thing was different things about the weather. There's a Bitnet list available that comes via email, just like the one mentioned in Chapter 4. According to the *Everything* book, to get the list, you send email to

LISTSERV@vmd.cso.uiuc.edu

and join the list called WX_NATNL by typing

SUB WX_NATNL

in the body of the message.

This list gives the National Weather Service forecast for several cities. There are other weather lists available from this site, too; to get a list of them, send a mail message to the same address, with no subject, and the single line

list

in the body of the mail message.

Sports

There's a list for play-by-play sportscasts out there, too. It's at

LISTSERV@etsuadmn.bitnet

and the list is called PBP-L. (A lot of Bitnet lists end in -L.)

Food and Recipes

Archie found a few food and recipe lists. The Foodlore/Recipe Exchange list is at

> **LISTSERV@vtvm1.bitnet**

and join the list called EAT-L.

For a discussion of food and wine:

> **LISTSERV@cmuvm.bitnet**

and join the list called FOODWINE.

You can find a discussion of Japanese food and culture on

> **LISTSERV@jpnknu01.bitnet**

and join the list called J-FOOD-L.

Lists About Traveling

Here's a discussion about traveling in Europe:

> **LISTSERV@ptearn.bitnet**

and join the list called EUROTRAV.

Federal Jobs

This is the federal job bulletin board:

> **LISTSERV@dartcms1**

and join the list called FEDJOBS.

Films

Here are a couple of lists on films. This one is on filmmaking and reviews:

> **LISTSERV@itesmvf1**

and the list is called FILM-L.

This one is a discussion list on film music:

> **LISTSERV@iubvm**

and join the list called FILMUS-L.

Etc.

Here's a discussion about Miles Davis, the late jazz trumpeter:

> **LISTSERV@hearn.bitnet**

and join the list called MILES.

FTP Sites

The following FTP sites have a ton of files for all different computers, including MS-DOS, Mac, Amiga, and Unix machines.

> **archive.umich.edu**
>
> **sumex-aim.stanford.edu**

oak.oakland.edu

ftp.sura.net

quartz.rutgers.edu

Electronic Magazines

Several people publish online magazines that you can have sent to your email address automatically. These come and go very rapidly, though, so instead of listing them here, lists can be found in the alternate newsgroup alt.zines.

Telnet Sites

The *Everything* book explained that there are a lot of computers on the Internet that hold tons of information on a certain topic; such information banks are called *databases*. These databases are accessible through Telnet; you can log into these computers and access the information in the database.

Weather

Archie found another place to get the weather. The *Everything* book says to telnet to

aeolus.rap.ucar.edu

and log in as

weather

with password

orknot

(Cute, thought Archie.) Yet another place for weather reports is

telnet downwind.sprl.umich.edu 3000

Or check the National Oceanic and Atmospheric Administration weather report at

telnet esdim1.nodc.noaa.gov

logging in as

noaddir

There was also a database on earthquake information at

telent bison.cc.buffalo.edu

Log in as guest. Another place to get earthquake information is at

telnet geophys.washington.edu

logging in as

quake

with password

quake

More on Telnet

For political stock market information:

telnet iem.biz.uiowa.edu

And there's a NASA database at all these places:

telnet ned.ipac.caltech.edu

(log in as ned);

telnet nssdc.gsfc.nasa.gov

(log in as nodis);

telnet nssdca.gsfc.nasa.gov

(also log in as nodis).

You can get more space information at these places:

telnet spacelink.msfc.nasa.gov
telnet spacemet.phast.umass.edu

Information about the Hubble space telescope is at

telnet stis.nsf.gov

(log in as public).

There's a history database at

telnet ukanaix.cc.ukans.edu

(log in as history).

A science database is at

telnet pldsg3.gsfc.nasa.gov

(log in as FIFEUSER). Remember that logins are case-sensitive!

Sports

Sports schedules for different leagues are available via Telnet.

NBA:

telnet culine.colorado.edu 859

NHL:

telnet culine.colorado.edu 860

MLB:

telnet culine.colorado.edu 862

NFL:

telnet culine.colorado.edu 863

And there's a computerized dictionary at

telnet wombat.doc.ic.ac.uk

(log in as guest).

Mail

In the *Everything* book Archie discovered email addresses for the president and vice president of the United States:

> **mail president@whitehouse.gov**
> **mail vicepresident@whitehouse.gov**

The *Everything* book also explained how to send email to friends who have accounts on some of the big online systems.

CompuServe

To send email to a person on CompuServe, suppose this person has CompuServe ID number 12345,1234. You would send email over the Internet to

> **12345.1234@compuserve.com**

Notice that the comma in the ID number has been replaced by a period.

Delphi

To send email to a person on Delphi, send it to

> **username@delphi.com**

where **username** is the name your friend uses to log in.

America Online

To send email to a person on America Online, send it to

> **username@aol.com**

where, again, **username** is the name your friend uses to log in.

BIX

Sending mail to a person on BIX works similarly to Delphi and America Online. Send the mail to

> **username@bix.com**

where **username** is the person's login name.

GEnie

To send mail to someone on GEnie, which is owned by General Electric (hence the GE in the name), send it to

> **username@genie.geis.com**

where **username** is the person's login name.

Prodigy

When sending email to a person on Prodigy, send it to

> **userid@prodigy.com**

where **userid** is the ID the person uses for logging in (usually a cryptic sequence of letters and numbers).

Universities

The *Everything* book explained that almost every university in the United States, and many elsewhere, are on the Internet. The best place to find the email addresses for universities is to watch the Usenet group soc.college.

Call Information!

Archie read in the *Everything* book that if you want to send email to somebody and don't know their email address, there are a few different ways to get it. One way is if you happen to see a posting on Usenet by someone who works at the same company where this person works, you might try sending email to that person asking for your friend's email address.

Another thing you can do, if you know the site where the person is, is to send email to **postmaster@site**, where site is the name of the site, such as super.geeks.com:

> **mail postmaster@super.geeks.com**

Note that a real person will read this, so you can say whatever you want, but it's best to be friendly and polite.

You can also purchase books that list what seems like a million email addresses of people; but the author of the *Everything* book mentioned that he had little luck with these, since they are so incomplete.

One particularly useful way to find an email address is through a service provided by MIT. If the person has posted anything on Usenet, a certain computer at

Figure 10-1 Rain, sleet, and snow can't prevent the postmaster from finding you

MIT will probably have the address, because this computer tracks all the From lines of all Usenet postings.

To try this, suppose you're trying to find someone with the last name Newton. Try sending email to

mail-server@rtfm.mit.edu

Leave the subject blank

subject:

and for the body of the message type:

send usenet-addresses/Newton

When MIT's server receives the message, it will run a search across the Internet and send you the results.

The *Everything* book warned that this server still may not find the person you're looking for. That doesn't mean the person isn't out there; it just means the server can't find the person.

The book also warned that you simply may not be able to find someone's Internet address short of calling him or her on the phone and asking for it!

The Finger Command

Archie found a chapter called "Finger" in the *Everything* book. It was long and boring, and spent a lot of time on how Unix works. But he was able to get some interesting facts out of the chapter. Apparently finger is a command for finding out information about users. You type **finger** followed by a username, the @ symbol, and a site name, and you'll get perhaps a screen full of information. The people logged into the computers that supply this information don't always give information about users, but information about other stuff. Here are some things you can try and see what happens. (The *Everything* book has a reminder that these change periodically, and these were working at the time the book was printed.)

adam@mtv.com

hotlist@mtv.com

magliaco@pilot.njin.net

nasanews.space.mit.edu

normg@halcyon.halcyon.com

Finding Cool Stuff

Various people on the Internet enjoy compiling "cool things" lists. These databases are generally available via FTP.

The author of the *Everything* book managed to find one that's kept at csd4.csd.uwm.edu by a user named yanoff. For information on getting the list, you can use finger:

yanoff@csd4.csd.uwm.edu

Or you can ftp to that site and get it:

> csd4.csd.uwm.edu

Once in, you can type

> cd /pub

and the file is called

> inet.services.txt.

CHAPTER 11

Gopher It!

CHAPTER 11

Gopher It!

Archie was frustrated. He had sent a reply to the person who posted the message about windsurfing, and he hadn't gotten a reply yet. But that's not what frustrated him. What frustrated him was that it's so difficult to find things on the Internet.

Archie felt the whole concept of the Internet itself really wasn't that difficult to understand, once you get a feel for how it works, with characters moving from one keyboard to another screen, and files moving from one computer to another. But it's difficult to find things. You need to know where you're headed before you can get there. It seems like you need to be handed a book listing everything that's out there, and only then can you find what you're looking for.

Suddenly there was a flash, and then the room became a tiny bit darker. Archie looked around the room, wondering if some magical elf had appeared to help him out. But there was nobody there—just a lamp on the other side of the room that had burned out. So much for a flash of inspiration. Fortunately, the lamp on his desk was still on.

But maybe there was an easier way around this.

He fired up the computer, dialed out to Simple Internet, and logged in. There was a mail message. It was from Veronica!

> **Hi, Archie!**
> **Hope all is going well.**
> **Gopher a short break — online, that is!**
>
> **Sincerely,**
> **Veronica**

Gopher a short break? That's a rather odd thing to say, thought Archie. But he knew better than to sweat over it. He was getting the hang of this thing. Gopher must be another Internet program.

He got out of the mail program and typed

> **gopher**

Sure enough! Something happened! The screen turned into this:

It's the One and Only Simple Internet Gopher Server!

Main Menu

—> 1. **Welcome to the Simple Internet Connection!**
   2. **All the Documentation for Simple Internet/**
   3. **Frequently Asked Questions About Simple Internet/**
   4. **Other Gophers/**
   5. **Other Stuff/**

Press ? for Help, q to Quit, u to go up

This looks easy, Archie thought. He pressed (1) and waited. Nothing happened. He pressed (ENTER). Nothing. He pressed (ENTER) again. Aha!

The following message appeared on the screen:

Welcome to the Simple Internet Connection! This server boasts a large array of stuff for the Internet, including

   - ftp
   - telnet
   - gopher
   - mail

and tons more! Have fun!

The main menu showed up again on the screen.

Well that was nice, thought Archie. He pressed (2), and again pressed (ENTER) twice. I wonder, he thought, why I have to press (ENTER) twice?

The following menu appeared:

Documentation Menu

—> 1. **Introduction to Gopher!**
   2. **More About Gopher**
   3. **Even More About Gopher**
   4. **More Information Than You'll Need (from the Everything Book)**

Press ? for Help, q to Quit, u to go up

Archie pressed (1) and then pressed (ENTER) twice. The following message appeared:

Introduction to Gopher!

The simplest (and only) documentation for the Simple Internet Gopher server.

Gopher is an easy way to get information off of the Simple Internet computer. Using gopher, you can get files from other computers, and run programs on other computers, without having to manually use Telnet or FTP—gopher does it for you!

Here's how it works. You just select a menu item by using the up and down arrow keys to move the —> pointer up and down

the menu and pressing Enter when the arrow points to the selection you want. Since this up and down stuff might not work on all computers, you can also type the number corresponding to the item you wish to select. After you type the number, you have to press Enter twice.

If you're in a menu and you want to go back to the previous menu, you can press "u" for up. That'll take you "up" to the previous menu.

There are lots of things that may appear in these menus. If there's a slash "/" following an item in a menu, selecting it will cause another menu to appear on your screen, and from there you can again choose any item. Otherwise it's probably a text file for viewing.

Note that those of us who run the computer here at the Simple Internet Connection chose what to put in the main menu and the menus that you get when you select an item in the main menu followed by a slash.

The same is true for other computers on the Internet. Those computers often have a gopher program running on them, and the system operators ("sysops") have chosen what to include in their menus.

But here's the cool thing about gopher. We've included in the fourth entry in the main menu an item called "Other Gophers." If you choose this item, you will get a list of several other computer systems that run gopher. If you choose one, we'll connect to that computer over the Internet, grab its gopher information, and give you yet another menu. That menu is the same menu you'd see if you logged onto that computer directly and ran gopher.

If by chance you have a copy of the book called "Everything You Ever Wanted to Know About the Internet, and Then Some," you might look in Chapter 158, page 5,230, Figure 1536-C for an interesting illustration on this.

Archie grabbed the *Everything* book and turned to page 5,230. Sure enough, there was an illustration. It's shown here as Figure 11-1.

Archie then tried it. He pressed Ⓤ to leave the Documentation menu and return to the main menu. He pressed ④, for Other Gophers. The following menu appeared:

Other Gophers

—> 1.   The Information Unlimited BBS of Antarctica/
     2.   Difficult Internet Connection/
     3.   Libraries/

Press ? for Help, q to Quit, u to go up

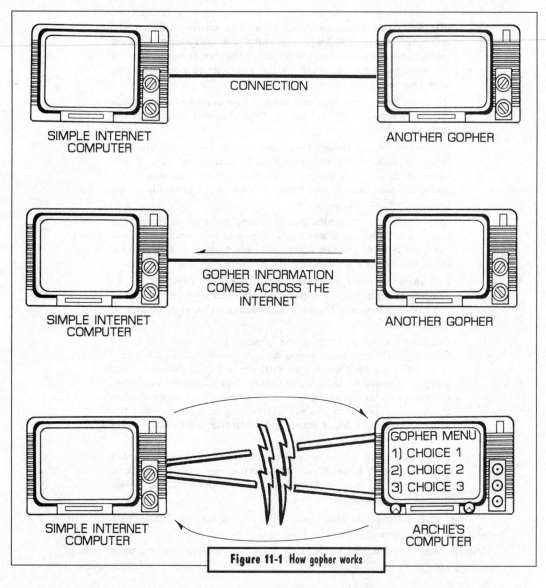

Figure 11-1 How gopher works

Archie pressed ⊙ twice to point to 3. The screen now looked like this:

Other Gophers

1. **The Information Unlimited BBS of Antarctica/**
2. **Difficult Internet Connection/**
—> 3. **Libraries/**

Press ? for Help, q to Quit, u to go up

He pressed (ENTER).

The following menu appeared:

Library Gopher

—> 1.   Community College Library/
    2.   Law Library of U of Q/
    3.   Medical Library U of Q/
    4.   Library of the State Penitentiary/

Press ? for Help, q to Quit, u to go up

Archie selected 2. The following appeared:

Law Library Gopher

    1.   Card Catalog
    2.   Online Sources (TEL)

Press ? for Help, q to Quit, u to go up

He didn't really want to look up anything at the law library, so he pressed Ⓤ. The Library Gopher menu appeared again. He pressed Ⓤ again, and the Other Gophers menu appeared. He pressed Ⓤ yet again, bringing up the main menu.

It occurred to Archie that when he was in the Other Gophers menu, and he selected Libraries, he probably connected to another computer without really knowing it. Or did he? He wasn't sure. Then when he chose Law Library, he figured he must have connected to the computer downtown at the law school's library, accessing that computer's gopher system. But he wasn't really sure. He decided to go to the Documentation menu and read a bit more. He pressed ②️ from the main menu to look at the Documentation menu.

Tunneling Deeper

When the Documentation menu appeared again, Archie pressed the Ⓓ, moving the —> pointer to the second position. The screen looked like this:

Documentation Menu

    1.   Introduction To Gopher!
—> 2.   More About Gopher
    3.   Even More About Gopher
    4.   More Information Than You'll Need (from the Everything Book)

Press ? for Help, q to Quit, u to go up

He pressed (ENTER), and the following message appeared on his screen:

More About Gopher

Great, you've decided to further your studies and learn even more about gopher!

Well, I have news for you. There's not a whole lot more! But there is a tad bit more, so let's get on with it.

First, when you choose an item that hooks you up to a gopher server on another computer, the Simple Internet computer gets

(continued on page 124)

(continued from page 123)

the information for that computer's menus and displays them nice and neat, just like they're part of our own menus.

When that happens, you may be presented with the opportunity to connect to yet another computer system's gopher. If you go for it, you will get yet another menu. This process can go on and on, until you're several levels deep with more and more menus. Using gopher, you can tunnel throughout almost the entire Internet, going from computer to computer, seeing menu after menu.

Note that one menu might bring you to another menu on the same computer you're currently connected to, or it might connect you to another computer. At first it might seem silly for you not to know where you are, but it actually simplifies things by keeping all the information in nice, neat menus that you can use to just pick things.

Incidentally, the gopher menus that you see in the book you're in will be different from the menus the readers see when they use gopher. Also, if their system doesn't have gopher, there are ways around that; these are explained at the end of the chapter of the book you're in.

So, Archie thought, I guess when I have a menu that came from another computer, and choose an item that connects me to yet another computer, I then connect to that next one. I guess this could go on and on and on. Then a thought struck him. The Simple Internet had a list of computers he could gopher to, and presumably those gopher servers would have lists of other gopher sites, too. I wonder, he thought, if the Simple Internet computer appears in any of those lists? Then I could sort of loop back, and end up where I started. That would be weird.

FTP and Telnet

Archie chose item 3 in the Documentation menu, Even More About Gopher. Things were coming pretty easy so far, so he wanted to learn as much as he could while he had the chance. The following appeared on his screen:

Even More About Gopher

Inside these menus, you will often be presented with items that aren't new menus; rather, they're text files. If you choose one of these text files from a menu that's really the gopher menu from some remote computer, the Simple Internet computer will do an FTP for you and pull the file across the Internet and display it on your screen. And this all happens without your even having to worry about it!

Sometimes, you'll choose an item that will result in a Telnet to another computer. When that happens you'll connect to a remote computer, just as if you telneted to it. Try it!

Figure 11-2 Gophering a file

Archie then chose the last item in the Documentation menu, called More Information Than You'll Need. As soon as he saw a bunch of math formulas appear on the screen, he waited until the Documentation Menu appeared and he chose item 3 again.

He again looked over item 3, Even More About Gopher. So apparently when he's off in gopher land (or is it gopher world? thought Archie) and he's connected to a computer, which is connected to a computer, which is connected to another computer, he can eventually pull a file back to the Simple Internet computer, just like he did a few chapters back when learning about FTP. In fact, according to this last note, the gopher program actually uses FTP to do this.

Archie thought about it. Suppose you select a menu item that leads to a menu that's coming from another gopher server. Then from there you choose an item that leads to yet another gopher server's menu. That means you're logged into the Simple Internet computer, which is running gopher, which in turn is getting a menu from a computer, which got the menu from yet another computer. And on that last computer is an item for a file you want such as windsurfer. The gopher program would then go for it, similar to Figure 11-2. You select it, and the Simple Internet uses FTP to go get the file and bring it back and print it on your screen.

He decided to try it. He got back to the main menu and then the Other Gophers menu. From there he chose the Difficult Internet Connection. The following menu appeared on his screen:

Difficult Internet Gopher Server

—> 1.   **Entire text of Designing RISC-based Computer Systems**
2.   **FTP!**
3.   **Einstein's Theory of General Relativity—a critical analysis**
4.   **Using complex differential equations to solve everyday problems**
5.   **How to use an earthquake measuring device in reverse**

Press ? for Help, q to Quit, u to go up

Archie chose 2. The following appeared:

Difficult Internet's FTP Gopher Menu

—> 1.   **Did you know . . .**
2.   **Our own FTP stuff!**

Press ? for Help, q to Quit, u to go up

He chose 1.

Did You Know . . .

That Sergio Rachmaninoff was only 19 when he composed his famous Prelude in C# Minor? Well, as it happens, I, the sysop for the Difficult Internet Connection was only 19 when I built my own RISC-based supercomputer. But that's not what I'm here to talk about. I'm here to talk about FTP.

If you choose item 2, you will be presented with a huge list of directories. These are the same as you would get if you were to ftp to this site, only instead of having to type dir to see it all, you'll get an actual menu! Gopher it! Yes, gopher makes it a lot simpler. That's why we prefer not to use it here at the Difficult Internet Connection. But you're welcome to use it.

The menu appeared again, and he chose 2, Our own FTP stuff! The following menu appeared:

FTP Stuff

1.   **bin/**
2.   **dev/**
3.   **etc/**
—> 4.   **pub/**
5.   **usr/**

Press ? for Help, q to Quit, u to go up

This was apparently the same as what Archie would see if he were to ftp to this computer and type dir. These were all the directories in the root. He selected 4, pub/, which is probably public stuff. The following menu appeared:

Directory of pub/

—> 1.   unix/
    2.   xwin/
    3.   msdos/
    4.   math/
    5.   physics/

Press ? for Help, q to Quit, u to go up

He chose 3, msdos. The following menu appeared:

Directory of pub/msdos

—> 1.   games/
    2.   text/
    3.   language/
    4.   system/

Press ? for Help, q to Quit, u to go up

He chose 1. The following appeared:

Directory of pub/msdos/games

—> 1.   readme
    2.   doom.zip
    3.   wolf3d.zip
    4.   tim.zip

Press ? for Help, q to Quit, u to go up

Archie already had all these games, so he pressed Ⓤ several times until he was all the way back to the main menu.

He went through so many menus, he started to forget that he ever left Simple Internet's gopher information and was getting information from other computers.

He chose Other Gophers, Libraries, and then Law Library. The following again appeared on his screen:

Law Library Gopher

    1.   Card Catalog
    2.   Online Sources (TEL)

Press ? for Help, q to Quit, u to go up

He guessed that TEL meant if he chose that item he'd end up telneting out. So he chose it. And sure enough, the following appeared on his screen:

Use login "Guest"
Trying 54.2.2.3 . . .
Connected to law.library.edu
Escape character is '^]'

login:

He didn't really feel like going through another Telnet session, so he held down the CTRL key and pressed Ⓙ. That got him out of the Telnet session, and the previous Law Library Gopher menu appeared again.

He pressed Ⓠ to get out of the gopher program.

No Gopher!

Archie was glancing through the *Everything* book, and he noticed the following:

> Some computers don't offer gopher services. If the computer you nor-
> mally use doesn't have gopher, but it does have Telnet, you can telnet
> to a system that has a public gopher client and run gopher from there.
> The two main places to do this are

> **telnet consultant.micro.umn.edu**

and

> **telnet ux1.cso.uiuc.edu**

Archie closed the book and decided to go to sleep.

CHAPTER 12

Special Interests

Archie just happened to log in, and found two email messages waiting for him. The first was from Max:

> **Dear Mr. Finger,**
>
> **Thank you for replying to the anonymous posting. You're learning these Internet concepts very well. Very well, indeed.**
>
> **Sincerely,**
>
> **Max Von Veign**

The second was from Gloria:

> **Hi Archie,**
>
> **This is Gloria. I'm sorry you were misled. Ignore all mail from Max. He's the bad guy here, not me.**
>
> **Here are some possibilities to help you find the missing person. Gather up a list of as many FTP sites and Telnet sites you can find that offer special interest databases.**
>
> **Once you've compiled the list, send it to me and I'll see if I can use it to help you find the missing person.**
>
> **And beware: Regard Max as the enemy.**
>
> **Sincerely,**
>
> **Gloria**

Oh, that's just great, thought Archie. Now I don't know who to trust. Gloria? Veronica? Or this new guy, Max? It's clear somebody is the bad guy. But who can I trust?

He decided not to trust anybody. He'd go ahead and gather up that list for Gloria, but while sending it to her, he'd also send it off to Max. That should have some interesting results.

Let's see, thought Archie, special interest groups. I guess the first place to look is in some of these books I have. Either that or see what's out there, online. But is that the best way? He couldn't believe it would be. With all that information out there on the Internet, weren't there some computers that kept track of all the information?

He grabbed the *Everything* book and glanced through the enormous table of contents. Eventually he found something that might be what he was looking for: a chapter called "Finding Things."

He turned to the page and was shocked to see his name and Veronica's name both in there. Apparently both archie and veronica are the names of programs.

First he read about archie.

Archie

The *Everything* book explained that both archie and veronica are programs for tracking things down easily on the Internet. Archie is for finding FTP sites; veronica assists in using gopher.

Archie helps by searching throughout the Internet for files that you request; it will come back with the names of all the FTP sites it finds that carry the requested file.

Archie decided to try out this archie thing. While he was logging onto the Simple Internet computer, he was thinking how intriguing it was that someone named an Internet program after him. But, on further thought, he had the paranoid feeling that perhaps it was the other way around.

Once on the Simple Internet computer, he typed

archie

and the computer responded with

archie: command not found

Well, he thought to himself, that didn't work. Now what? He looked in the *Everything* book and saw a list of so-called archie servers. Apparently not all Internet computers have an archie program. That was certainly the case with the Simple Internet computer. So Archie figured he probably had to telnet to one of those archie-server computers. Then he could run archie.

Here's the list of archie servers given in the *Everything* book:

archie.rutgers.edu	(Rutgers University in New Jersey)
archie.sura.net	(SURAnet in Maryland)
archie.unl.edu	(University of Nebraska in Lincoln)
archie.ans.net	(ANS archie server in New York)
archie.au	(Australia)
archie.funet.fi	(Finland)
archie.doc.ic.ac.uk	(England)
archie.cs.huji.ac.il	(Israel)
archie.wide.ad.jp	(Japan)
archie.ncu.edu.tw	(Taiwan)

The *Everything* book suggested you telnet to the closest one, if possible. That means if you're in New Jersey, it's best to try telneting first to archie.rutgers.edu, rather than, say, archie.wide.ad.jp.

Archie typed

    telnet archie.rutgers.edu

and the next thing he knew he was at the archie server. There was the usual stuff on the screen, followed by a login prompt. He logged in as archie—not because that's his name, but because that's what you log in as when you're telneting to an archie server.

    login: archie

Then there was an archie prompt:

    archie>

The *Everything* book explained that with archie you can specify some letters to search for in a file name, and archie will find as many FTP sites as it can that have a file name containing those letters. For example, Archie wanted to find all FTP sites that had a file with the word "windsurf" in it.

There are a few different ways archie can search—one is for any file that has the requested word somewhere in it. For example, if the word to search for is "wind," then archie could find files called, say, windsurf, or windy, or abcwindxyz —anything, as long as the word "wind" is somewhere inside the file name. This is called the *substring* method.

Another kind of search is an exact match. Archie can be told to find only files that are called exactly wind. So windsurf, windy, and abcwindxyz wouldn't show up in this kind of search. This search method is called the *exact* method.

The first thing archie needs is the type of search to do. So Archie typed, as suggested by the *Everything* book,

    set search sub

This tells it to gear up for a substring search. To begin the search, Archie typed

    prog wind

The prog command tells archie to begin the search. The search can take several minutes. Archie waited a few moments, and eventually saw something appear on his screen. Here's a partial list of what he saw:

```
Host whitechapel.media.mit.edu  (18.85.0.125)
Last updated 11:04 25 Nov 1993

    Location: /pub/SunOSpatches
         FILE  -rw-rw-r—  50220 bytes 23:00 9 Oct 1990
flush_windows.tar.Z


Host ftp.cis.upenn.edu  (130.91.6.8)
Last updated 11:03 12 Nov 1993

    Location: /pub/dsl/Amarnath
         FILE  -rw-r—r—  1201 bytes 00:00 9 Jul 1991
abstract.time-window.tex.Z
```

(continued on page 134)

(continued from page 133)

      FILE -rw-r—r— 299199 bytes 00:00 9 Jul 1991 time-window.ps.Z

      FILE -rw-r—r—   583 bytes 00:00 9 Jul 1991 title.time-window.tex.Z

Host janus.library.cmu.edu (128.2.21.7)

Last updated 11:03 12 Nov 1993

    Location: /next/Admin/UpgradePrep.app

      FILE -rwxrwxr-x 493547 bytes 00:00 25 Jun 1992 WindowServer.Z

    Location: /next/Apps/DarkForest.app/English.lproj

      DIRECTORY drwxrwxr-x 512 bytes 10:49 9 May 1993 FileWindow.nib

    Location: /next/Apps/TickleServices1.01/TickleServices.app/Online/Menus/Menus.rtfd

      FILE -rw-rw-r— 442 bytes 03:10 29 Jun 1993 Windows.tiff

    Location: /next/Apps/TickleServices1.02mab/TickleServices.app/Online/Menus/Menus.rtfd

      FILE -rw-rw-r— 442 bytes 20:10 29 Jun 1993 Windows.tiff

    Location: /next/Library/NeXTanswers/NEXTSTEP_In_Focus/InFocusSpring1993/1131_Tips.rtfd

      FILE -rwxrwxr-x 8052 bytes 00:31 3 Jun 1993 BugNeXTmainWindow2.tiff

So now Archie knew which FTP sites had files with the substring "wind" in their names.

Archie made a note of a few of the files. He saw that some FTP sites had the same file. That was fine; he could then ftp to any of those sites to get the file if he wanted it.

He then decided to do an exact search, just for fun. He had to tell archie to gear up for an exact search by typing

    set search exact

He then typed

    prog windsurf

to find all the files out there called windsurf.

When Archie pressed ⟨ENTER⟩ and waited a while, eventually, to his disappointment, he saw:

    # No matches were found.

Apparently it couldn't find any files called *exactly* windsurf. Of course, if there's a file called windsrf, for instance, without the *u*, it wouldn't show up in this search. Archie decided it's best to search on a substring; that way there's a better chance of finding what you're looking for.

There's yet another kind of search, Archie discovered. It's called the *subcase* method. This works very similarly to the substring search method, except it's case-sensitive. That means, if you search on "wind," it won't find, say, a file called Windy, because the *W* is uppercase in the file name, while it's lowercase in the requested substring. To turn on this type of search, type

set search subcase

Archie then decided to read about veronica.

Veronica

Veronica, which supposedly stands for Very Easy Rodent-Oriented Net-wide Index to Computerized Archives, is a program for finding things in gopher. The way it works is you specify a word to search for, and veronica searches through the Internet, gathering up items from gopher menus, and compiles them into a single gopher menu for you to use. Veronica demonstrates what she does in Figure 12-1.

Archie decided to try it out. He got on the Simple Internet computer and typed

veronica

Figure 12-1 Veronica gathers up gopher menus

Once again the computer responded with

veronica: command not found

He looked in the *Everything* book and realized that the usual way to get to veronica is through a gopher server. So he got onto gopher, and the familiar menu appeared:

It's the One and Only Simple Internet Gopher Server!

Main Menu

—> 1.   **Welcome to the Simple Internet Connection!**
    2.   **All the Documentation for Simple Internet/**
    3.   **Frequently Asked Questions About Simple Internet/**
    4.   **Other Gophers/**
    5.   **Other Stuff/**

Press ? for Help, q to Quit, u to go up

He didn't see an entry mentioning veronica. He'd been through the Documentation menu, as well as the Welcome menu. The Other Gophers menu connected him to lots of other gophers, and from there he could go out into gopherspace and tunnel through nearly the entire Internet. It might take too long going that route to find a veronica program, so Archie chose 5, just for kicks.

Sure enough, that's where it was:

Other Stuff

—> 1.   **Our FTP stuff**
    2.   **Veronica**

Press ? for Help, q to Quit, u to go up

He pressed ⊙ and then (ENTER). The following appeared:

Search Gopherspace Using Veronica

Enter words to search for:

Archie typed **windsurfing** and then pressed (ENTER). There was a pause of a few minutes, and the following appeared on his screen, just like a gopher menu:

—> 1.   **Windsurf BBS/**
    2.   **How to Windsurf**
    3.   **Best Places to Windsurf**

Archie knew that the first item would result in another menu, while the other two were text files. He had no idea where those text files were, but he trusted that now that he had a gopher menu, gopher would go ahead and get the files if he asked for them.

A List of Special Interest Stuff

Archie used archie and veronica, along with just trying different gopher sites, to compile this list for Gloria.

If you're interested in Macs, try

telnet amdalinz.edvz.uni-linz.ac.at

If you're interested in PCs, here's Microsoft's FTP site:

ftp ftp.microsoft.com

For lots of MS-DOS software, the following are good sites:

ftp oak.oakland.edu
ftp ftp.sura.net

In the /pub/nic directory, try

ftp quartz.rutgers.edu

If you're interested in medicine, try the following site for a whole bunch of medical information:

gopher eja.anes.hscsyr.edu

For cancer information:

telnet txcancer.mda.uth.tmc.edu

Log in as TCDC.

For assistance in finding disability services:

telnet bongo.cc.utexas.edu or telnet

If you're interested in the economy, finance, and the stock market:

telnet netec.mcc.ac.uk

Log in as netec. Or try

gopher infopath.ucsd.edu

and select News & Services and then Economic Bulletin Board.

If you're interested in careers and education, try the following site for the Career Center Online:

gopher gopher.msen.com

To search for jobs:

telnet career.com

For information on scholarships:

telnet fedix.fie.com

If you're interested in law and government, the following gives you information about Supreme Court rulings:

ftp ftp.cwru.edu

For lots of law information:

ftp sulaw.law.su.oz.au

and look in the directory /pub/law.

Here's how you can find out about getting government documents over email,

mail info@ace.esusda.gov

with

SEND HELP

for the message body.

If you're interested in science, here's the National Archaeological Database Online System:

> **telnet cast.uark.edu**

Log in as nadb.

> To see a periodic table:

> **telnet camms2.caos.kun.nl**

> For information on particle physics:

> **telnet muse.lbl.gov**

Log in as pdg_public. This is the Lawrence Berkeley Laboratory, Particle Data Group.

> For information about behavior relating to music:

> **telnet mila.ps.uci.edu**

This is the Music and Science Information Computer Archive.

> If you're interested in amateur radio:

> **ftp world.std.com**

Look in the directory pub/hamradio.

Done for the Day

As Archie was ready to quit for the day, something occurred to him. A few chapters back he used the finger command to look up information on users. Why couldn't he use finger to find out about Gloria, Max, and Veronica the person? He first tried Gloria:

> **finger gloria@super.geeks.com**

After a short pause, he saw the following:

> **Gloria Strysdale. Owner of Supergeeks, Inc., a consulting firm located on 563 Elm.**

Archie considered that. Owner? Of Supergeeks? Wasn't that who he was supposed to be looking for all along? But he thought it was a man, for one thing. And he thought the person was missing. Gloria's been around.

It occurred to him that he didn't know where she was now. But where was Supergeeks? At 563 Elm? That's the house he and Veronica were in when the mystery began.

He wondered if perhaps Veronica was involved even more than he had first suspected. Her email is coming from a Simple Internet account, but maybe she also has an account at Supergeeks. Archie typed

> **finger veronica@super.geeks.com**

and after a short pause saw

> **Newest hired employee! Let's everyone welcome her!**

No way, thought Archie. She's now working there? Did she resign from the accounting firm? When did that happen? And where was she *now*, for that matter?

He then typed

finger imgreat@covert.com

and saw

This is the computer system for Covert Consulting, Inc.
We're the world's greatest consulting firm, even better than
Supergeeks! imgreat is the computer name for our owner, Max
Von Veign.

No kidding, thought Archie.

CHAPTER 13

Fun Things

Fun Things

Archie was really starting to get into this Internet thing, so he decided to put the whole mystery on hold.

When he had been searching for cool things, he also found some fun things. Here's a list of what he found, along with some samplings from *Everything You Ever Wanted to Know About the Internet (and Then Some)*.

Online Games

There are many games available to play online through Telnet. The game runs on the remote computer, and you interact with it from your own computer. Most of these games are multiplayer versions, and you can talk to other people who are logged into the system and playing the game.

Othello

To play Othello, type

telnet faust.uni-paderborn.de 5000

You will be prompted for a login name to use during that session; it can be pretty much anything you want, and you can use a different name next time you log in. Type

help

to get instructions and

quit

to quit.

Backgammon

For backgammon, you can telnet to FIBS (First Internet Backgammon Server):

telnet fraggel65.mdstud.chalmers.se 4321

Log in as guest. You will be given instructions on how to register. When you register, you will be asked for a username; use this same username the next time you log in.

Chess and Scrabble

To play chess, type

> telnet rafael.metiu.ucsb.edu 5000

Or, to play scrabble:

> telnet next2.cas.muohio.edu 7777

Go

The Oriental game Go is available at any of these places:

> telnet bsdserver.ucsf.edu

> telnet hellspark.wharton.upenn.edu 6969

Log in as guest. Type **register** to sign up. Type **quit** to get out.

Downloadable Graphics and Games

The following sites have lots of games, graphics, and a ton of other stuff available. To use these, retrieve a copy with FTP. To look at the graphic images after you've pulled them down to your computer, you may need special graphics software. Such software is either available commercially or can be downloaded. In some cases the software may already be on your computer.

> ftp wuarchive.wustl.edu

> ftp sunset.cse.nau.edu

Note that the different file names will end with different sets of letters denoting the type of graphics file. For instance, a file that ends in .GIF (pronounced "jif," like the brand of peanut butter) is a certain type of graphics file, and .BMP (pronounced either "bump" or "bee-em-pee") is another type of graphics file.

Fun Fingers

This finger shows some fun trivia:

> finger cyndiw@magnus1.com

Other Fun Stuff

There's lots of fun stuff at these sites:

> ftp quartz.rutgers.edu

> ftp cathouse.org

> telnet astro.temple.edu 12345

> telnet argo.temple.edu 12345

Talking to Others

The *Everything* book mentions something called Internet Relay Chat (IRC). It explains that there are computers set up where several people can telnet to the same computer and talk to each other in "real time," as they say, almost like Figure 13-1. In other words, everything they type appears on your screen, and everything you type appears on their screens. To try this out, here are a few places to telnet to. The first one is a chat server if your terminal program supports something called TermCap.

telnet clique.cdf.utoronto.ca 6668	log in as irc
telnet clique.cdf.utoronto.ca 6669	log in as irc

If these don't work right, here are some others:

telnet bwrt.wb.psu.edu	log in as irc
telnet debra.dgbt.doc.ca	log in as chat
telnet exuokmax.ecn.uoknor.edu 6677	log in as irc
telnet hastur.cc.edu	log in as irc
telnet irc.demon.co.uk	log in as irc
telnet ircd.demon.co.uk 6666	log in as irc
telnet irc.nsysu.edu.tw	log in as irc, with password irc
telnet irc.tuzvo.sk 6668	log in as irc

(continued on page 146)

Figure 13-1 "Real time" talk with IRC

(continued from page 145)

telnet marble.bu.edu 2010	log in as guest
telnet proj.jpl.nasa.gov	log in as irc
telnet sci.dixie.edu 6677	log in as irc
telnet speedway.net 7777	log in as guest
telnet upsun.up.edu 4000	log in as guest

The *Everything* book warns that these were functional when the *Everything* book was written; but these chat servers tend to be shut down and new ones put up periodically, so when the reader tries them, some may not work anymore.

MUDs

Many systems out there let you log in and interact with other users, much like the IRCs mentioned above, except everyone is playing roles in a dungeon game. These are called Multi-User Dungeons, or MUDs.

Systems that carry MUDs come and go quickly, so the best place to find out about them is by watching the Usenet group rec.games.mud.announce.

CHAPTER 14

Or So the Story Goes . . .

Archie arrived at 563 Elm Street, which was the same house he and Veronica were in when the mystery started. Only this time the house wasn't quiet. There was lots of noise coming from it. He heard a phone ring, and several voices.

He approached the front door. There was a sign on it; that certainly wasn't there last time he was at this house. It said:

Supergeeks, Inc.

Below it was another sign:

Welcome to Our World Headquarters!

Archie walked in the front door. The place looked similar to before, except there were lots of people all moving about, talking about computers. Gloria appeared from around a corner.

"Congratulations!" she yelled.

He jumped back.

"No, I'm serious!"

Several other people came up to him. They were all congratulating him.

"You found me!" said Gloria. "Come with me." She grabbed his hand and pulled. He followed behind her, her hand never loosening up. She led him down a hallway, down some stairs into the basement, and into a little room. There was a second door at the other end of the room, and through the door Archie could see the library where he and Veronica had first found the *Everything* book and the trapdoor. Archie grinned, wondering if anybody had found the broken chalice.

"Hello, Archie."

He looked to his left. "Veronica!" he said. "What are you doing here?"

"I think I'll let Gloria explain."

"Sit down," said Gloria, as she sat down behind a desk. "We have some paperwork to fill out. But first, you need an explanation."

Archie sat down in a chair in front of Gloria's desk.

"First of all," said Gloria, "I want to say you've done a wonderful job of learning all about the Internet. We've been looking for someone who has the detective skills that you do, and who can learn things as quickly as you can. We'd like to offer you a job as our Internet Investigator. Anytime anybody needs help finding anything on the Internet, you can have the honor of assisting them."

"Uhhh . . ." Archie didn't know what to say. He looked at Veronica. She was nodding.

"Perhaps," continued Gloria, "we should get right to the formal offer. How does a six-figure salary sound?"

Archie felt his heart skip a beat. "Um . . . is this for real?"

"It sure is," said Veronica. "You should see what they offered me, just to be your assistant."

"You're gonna work for me?" asked Archie.

"I take it," said Gloria, "you're accepting the position?"

"Well, um . . . Sure!"

"Great! We'll get to the paperwork shortly. But before you're officially indoctrinated, you have to know about some Internet legends."

Veronica said, "I'll tell you the first one. Nobody knows if this really happened, and most people figure it didn't. But the story goes that somebody once went into a restaurant, and after eating a meal, enjoyed a chocolate chip cookie for dessert."

"Wait a minute," said Archie. "What does this have to do with the Internet?"

Gloria said, "It's just one of the many stories every Internet traveler must know."

Veronica continued, "The person liked the cookie so well, he—or was it she—asked if the recipe was available. The server said 'Yes, it's available for two-fifty.' 'Well, put it on my credit card,' said the patron. The server did so, and presented the patron with the recipe. But later that month, when the patron got the credit card bill, he—or was it she—was shocked to see a charge of two hundred and fifty dollars, not two dollars and fifty cents. So she vowed to get even by giving the recipe to everybody who would take it. And she started by posting it on the Internet. Sometimes in Usenet when you see people talking about the story, someone will give a recipe. Apparently there's really a recipe out there, and I've heard it makes pretty good chocolate chip cookies. But nobody so far has claimed to be the person who was faced with the two hundred and fifty dollar recipe. Most people figure it never happened."

Gloria then began. "The next story is about a dying boy. Sooner or later you'll probably come across a posting where someone says there's a little boy dying and he wants to get into the *Guinness Book of World Records* for receiving the most cards. Well, that was a few years ago, and the boy has recovered, and he has since made it into the record book. So don't send a card, because he and his family are sick of receiving all those cards."

"The third story," said Veronica, "is about get-rich-quick schemes. You're bound to find postings and files about a man who had his car repossessed, but later found a way to make a million dollars. It's a pyramid scheme, and it's highly illegal. It involves replacing your own name with someone else's at the bottom of the letter, and sending a certain amount of money to the other people listed on the letter. You then send the letter off to five people, and they each do the same thing. But don't do it. It's illegal, and we don't need you going to jail. We need you here!"

Archie was only half-listening, while he was looking at a large computer system on the desk where Gloria was sitting. This place must have a pretty big budget, he thought to himself.

Suddenly Gloria stood up. "I'll go get Sally from Human Resources, and she'll get you squared away with all your tax forms. We've already taken the liberty of emailing your resignation to the accounting firm. Unfortunately, they want you to work for the rest of this week, but that shouldn't be a problem." She pointed to the desk she had been sitting at. "Meanwhile you can start setting up your desk."

She left the room.

Archie looked at Veronica. "So this is gonna be my office?"

"That's right, boss." She smiled and turned the computer on. The screen said

Welcome to the Simple Internet Connection. Your sysop is

Archie Finger.

As of yesterday, this system is owned and operated by
Supergeeks, Inc.

Archie reached down and shut the computer off. "Let's go get a bagel, instead. I need a break from the Internet."

"So do I," said Veronica.

They headed up the stairs and on to the 24-hour bagel shop.

Glossary

Archie
A program used for finding FTP files and their locations on the Internet. After archie finds a file, FTP can be used to retrieve it.

Bitnet
A special network that many list servers are on.

BTW
An acronym for by the way.

FTP
A program used for connecting to other computers on the Internet and transferring files. FTP stands for File Transfer Protocol.

Gopher
A menu-based program used for connecting from computer to computer to computer on the Internet.

IMHO
An acronym for either in my honest opinion or in my humble opinion.

Internet
The collective of thousands of computers across the world, all connected together.

List server
A program that handles mailing lists. Usually these mailing lists are for the purpose of discussion groups. You can send mail to everyone on the mailing list by sending it to the name of the list at the site where LISTSERV sits.

LISTSERV
The name of the list server that runs on IBM mainframe computers. This is the most common list server on the Internet.

Mailing list
A list of people maintained by a computer.

Menu

A set of text that appears on the screen, usually as a numbered or lettered list. Generally it's used in a program where you can respond by typing the number or letter corresponding to the item in the list you wish to choose.

Post

To write a Usenet or Bitnet list message and send it out on the Internet for everyone to see.

Poster

The person who posted a particular message.

Remote

A computer directly or indirectly connected to the computer you're using.

RTFM

An acronym for read the manual.

Shell

A program that lets you type in words and press (ENTER) to start programs or get directory listings.

Telnet

A program used for running programs on another computer on the Internet, and seeing the program's output on your own.

Unix

A certain set of programs that run on many computers on the Internet. This is similar but separate from DOS, for instance.

Veronica

A program used for searching out gopher sites and building gopher menus.

Appendix

telnet

To use telnet, type

telnet site

where site is the name of the computer you wish to connect to. You will probably be asked for a login name and password; if you don't have one you may not be able to proceed. However, you might try typing guest for the login name, and try leaving the password blank.

ftp

To use ftp type

ftp site

where site is the name of the computer you wish to connect to. Unless somebody has given you a legal login and password for this computer, you will need to use anonymous for the login name, and your email address for the password. (If you get a message telling you you're not allowed to login, then chances are this ftp site isn't open to the general public.)

Inside ftp, you may use the following commands:

 ascii
to tell both computers the next transfer is for a text file

 binary
to tell both computers the next transfer is not a text file

 get filename
to copy the file from the remote computer to the computer you're logged into

 dir
to see a list of files in the current directory and

 cd directory
where directory is a directory name to change to a different directory.

Gopher

To start gopher, type

> **gopher**

Once inside the menu, either use the arrow keys to move the pointer up and down (on some computers that might not work) or type the number for the menu item, followed by a return. (You may have to press return twice.)

Mail

To read your mail, type

> **mail**

If you have mail, you will be given a list of mail messages.
To send a mail message, type

> **mail user@site**

where user@site is the username and site address of the person you're sending email to.

nn

To start the nn newsreader, type

> **nn**

When in selection mode,

 To choose an item to be read, press the lowercase letter next to the item.

 (SHIFT)-(Z) takes you immediately to reading mode.

 (SPACEBAR) takes you to the next page.

 (<) takes you to the previous page.

 (SHIFT)-(G) lets you choose another newsgroup.

When in reading mode,

 (SPACEBAR) takes you to the next page.

 (BACKSPACE) takes you to the previous page (Mac users can use (DELETE)).

 (P) takes you to the previous article.

 (N) takes you to the next article.

 (=) takes you back to selection mode.

(F) lets you write a follow-up message.

: **post** lets you enter a new message with a new subject.

Index

Books have a substantial influence on the destruction of the forests of the Earth. For example, it takes 17 trees to produce one ton of paper. A first printing of 30,000 copies of a typical 480-page book consumes 108,000 pounds of paper which will require 918 trees!

Waite Group Press™ is against the clear-cutting of forests and supports reforestation of the Pacific Northwest of the United States and Canada, where most of this paper comes from. As a publisher with several hundred thousand books sold each year, we feel an obligation to give back to the planet. We will therefore support and contribute a percentage of our proceeds to organizations which seek to preserve the forests of planet Earth.

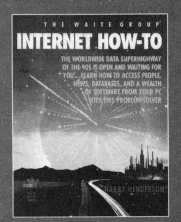
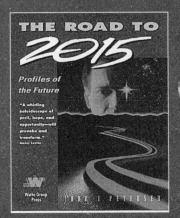
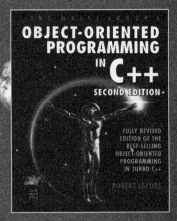

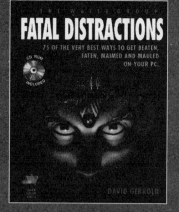
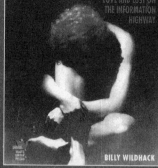

SATISFACTION REPORT CARD

Please fill out this card if you wish to know of future updates to *Simple Internet*, or to receive our catalog.

Company Name: _____

Division/Department: _____   Mail Stop: _____

Last Name: _____ First Name: _____ Middle Initial: _____

Street Address: _____

City: _____ State: _____ Zip: _____

Daytime telephone: (   ) _____

Date product was acquired: Month _____ Day _____ Year _____ Your Occupation: _____

Overall, how would you rate *Simple Internet*?
- ☐ Excellent
- ☐ Very Good
- ☐ Good
- ☐ Fair
- ☐ Below Average
- ☐ Poor

What did you like MOST about this book? _____
_____

What did you like LEAST about this book? _____
_____
_____

How did you use this book (problem-solver, tutorial, reference...)?
_____

What is your level of computer expertise?
- ☐ New
- ☐ Dabbler
- ☐ Hacker
- ☐ Power User
- ☐ Programmer
- ☐ Experienced Professional

Please describe your computer hardware:
Computer _____ Hard disk _____
5.25" disk drives _____ 3.5" disk drives _____
Video card _____ Monitor _____
Printer _____ Peripherals _____
Sound Board _____ CD ROM _____

What online services do you subscribe to?
- ☐ CompuServe
- ☐ BIX
- ☐ America Online
- ☐ Internet
- ☐ Delphi
- ☐ GEnie

Where did you buy this book?
- ☐ Bookstore (name): _____
- ☐ Discount store (name): _____
- ☐ Computer store (name): _____
- ☐ Catalog (name): _____
- ☐ Direct from WGP   ☐ Other _____

What price did you pay for this book? _____

What influenced your purchase of this book?
- ☐ Recommendation
- ☐ Advertisement
- ☐ Magazine review
- ☐ Store display
- ☐ Mailing
- ☐ Book's format
- ☐ Reputation of Waite Group Press
- ☐ Other

How many computer books do you buy each year? _____

How many other Waite Group books do you own? _____

What is your favorite Waite Group book? _____
_____

Is there any program or subject you would like to see Waite Group Press cover in a similar approach? _____
_____
_____

Additional comments? _____
_____

Please send to: Waite Group Press
Attn: *Simple Internet*
200 Tamal Plaza
Corte Madera, CA 94925

☐ Check here for a free Waite Group catalog